BELLY BUTTON CHAMPAGNE POOLS

and all the gifts
this body gave me

HANNAH WALKER

Copyright © Hannah Walker 2025

All rights reserved.
Hannah Walker has asserted her moral right
under the Copyright, Designs & Patent Act 1988
and no part of this work may be reproduced in any way
without prior written consent of Hannah Walker.

ISBN 9781738510313

Cover design:
Hannah Walker
Cover fonts:
Personal Services by Daniel Hochard
imagex-fonts.com
Internal images & illustrations:
Hannah Walker

Also by Hannah Walker
Mess is Progress
www.hannahpoems.co.uk

CONTENT WARNING

The entirety of this book is based on the four decades of my personal existence as a (mostly able-bodied) woman. This covers many topics that you may or may not want to read about.

The overall tone of these pages is light-hearted and jovial. Therefore the following subjects are touched on, but not graphically depicted. They include, but are not limited to: body image, sexual harassment, racism & white privilege, alcohol & recreational drug use, sexuality, intimacy and self-exploration, major surgery, trauma.

Despite the mostly positive slant I take throughout, I am in no way negating the validity of struggles or endorsing of risky behaviours, that were the running theme of my youth as an impulsive and un-diagnosed Autistic with ADHD.

Reader discretion is advised

I am focussing on the tidbits that were fucking funny. Buckle up - you should be in for a relatable, refreshing and unfiltered read.

I swear a lot.

Contents

Vessel	**9**
Self love	11
Tenuous Link	**12**
Hammer Toes	**15**
Toe-in	18
Tiptoes	19
Happy arches	20
Grounding grass	22
Totem	23
Polish	24
Cuddle toes	25
Ridiculous Umbilicus	**26**
Lint-less	28
Champagne pools	29
Smile	30
Butterbats	31
Belly rocket	32
The Largest Organ	**34**
Bronzed	42
Goosebumps	43
Tattoos	44
Factory dupe revolt	50
Twisty wrists	52
Flesh	53
Powerhouse Pair	**54**
Sister defence	57
Safety lap	58
Mes jambes	59
Accident prone, adrenaline junky	60
Scandalous Ankles	**63**
Thankles	67
Heels	68
Sock asphyxiation	69
Hand Span	**70**
To hold	74
Master of arts	75

Art therapy	76
Handful	77
Leaf and thumb	79
Earth-side	83
Extroverted Sister-hands	84
Sausage Fingers	**86**
Feeding the ducks	89
Hand-picked	91
Mood	92
Sucker	93
Finger pilgrimage	96
Cool AF	98
Guard dropped	99
Exploration	100
Mud Manicure	101
Hair is Everything	**102**
13 reasons	105
Sex hair	107
Death by tweezers	108
Watching paint dry	109
Shower massacre	110
Contradiction	111
Magic brush	112
Fringe Regret	113
Wind whipped	114
Resting Bitch Face	**116**
Contrasting visage	119
Friend stamps	120
Mirror, mirror	121
Smurf	122
Third time's a charm	123
Bare faced liar	125
Mouth	**128**
Battle cries	130
Blessed be the safe foods	132
Chase	134
Word Vomit	135
Mouthgasms	139
Sabotaged By My Baby Box	**141**

Unspoken	145
Juxtapostion	147
Older brother	148
Russian dolls	149
Ovaries before brovaries	152
Week seven	154
Boobs Glorious Boobs	**159**
Disco boobs	164
Magic mammaries	168
Pillows	171
M&M nips	172
Polaroids	174
Bootylicious	**177**
Arse logic	181
Patriarchal Pants	184
Under-bum	186
Who Is She	**188**
My Vagina is…	190
Front-bum fire	193
Read my lips	194
Trusty Ticker	**197**
My first friend	200
You made a grug	201
Dick tracey	203
Every day I'm jostling	207
Matriarch	208
Day one	211
The big ten	212
Tit club	218
Care and Action	**220**
Platonic supersonic	231
Not transactional	232
Cranial Chronicles	**236**
Hello brain	240
What's on your mind?	242
Mindful Misophonia	243
Wonder	246
Profit and Loss	**249**
Acknowledgments	**253**

Vessel

My body is the least interesting thing about me. She is merely a vessel with which I conduct my life through. I love this body for what it brings me. Every touch, each adventure and everything in between.

Throughout my life I have been bombarded with images and expectations of what my body should be. As if by some weird reason, how it presents, it's shape, size and even its hairs are the only thing of any value. I never forget the horror of change, I felt with my body after having my first child at seventeen years old. No-one, literally not one person told me about what would happen. My stomach didn't just disappear straight after birth? What is this! I had stretch marks consuming my entire physical teenage self, from boobs to thighs and belly. I was mortified. One deep and meaningful, inebriated conversation with friends at around eighteen years old, I discovered that they all had stretch marks and they hadn't even had kids. Even a male friend had them on his back after a growth spurt upwards. It didn't make me love my *tiger stripes* (vom) but it did make me accept them as normal and ok.

Fast forward a couple of decades and I was sucked in temporarily by the 'body positivity' movement, however it simply never sat right with me. Ultimately, I do not look at my flaws and love them. I don't hate them either. I'm neither here nor there, I'm indifferent. If you do need a word or phrase to understand this feeling, I believe the term now coined is *body neutrality*. Moving away from talking about our physical bodies and appearance and just do what we bloody enjoy.

Acceptance.

Self love

self love
acceptance
of all of me
every inch
each hair
every limb
one by one
a celebration
of the whole
wonderful she

Tenuous Link

Writing can be as addictive as crack, albeit with a lot less soul-sucking consequences. Unless of course you are a troll tip-tapping keyboards to mansplain comment sections online, or any mogul-owned media outlet. I digress. Writing for me can be anything from a healing process, or a need to understand. Those collections of black symbols stood proud on bright pages, oftentimes are for fun and others for clarity. As a self-confessed over-thinker, I can even painstakingly deliberate on the perfect sentences to script in a simple birthday card. There is a visceral need to be able to pour myself into the ink, so that the receiver of said folded paper, can feel it too - verbs and adjectives smacking them in the heart through their eyeballs. It was therefore not much of a shock that after finishing and publishing my first book... I was hooked.

I knew the next time I put pen to paper, I wanted it to be a lot less serious and for the pages to be catalogued with joy. When I wrote *Mess is Progress*, it was a life line. One that I truly needed and turns out, I wasn't alone in that need. Wow, the connections with complete strangers blew my mind.

Like some kind of compulsion, I was over-flowing in this urge. This new-found need to collate warmth and delight. Preserve the contentment and revel in the daft nostalgia. I was chomping at the bit to essay into the ether once more. With an as yet, untouched, lined notebook in my hand - a drinks bottle under one armpit, pen between my teeth, sunglasses atop my head and headphones precariously balanced under the other arm - I tiptoed barefoot up the garden steps. Soaking the warmth through my toes from the stones charged by the summer sun. Inspired by the thought of finally downloading the kaleidoscope of tangents inside my brain to its new home in ink. I took a deep breath ready to begin. Cushions... I need cushions. A meticulous arrangement, it had to be just so. A writers den laid out on the lawn. The distant hum of a mower three gardens over, melting into the sounds of gossiping birds and frisky pigeons. I began to scribble away, sprawled out, zen, in my happy place.

Several pages in, I wracked my brain with what could possibly link the poetry together as a whole in this second book. It came to me that a tenuous link was organically forming across the chaotic pages of my notebook. *Mess is Progress* was a monologue of meeting my brain properly for the first time. This book, this is about re-introducing myself to my body and all the the gifts she gave.

Not one to shy away from projectile dumping my inner most thoughts into written words, I headed on in - feet first.

Hammer Toes

The weird little digits at the end of my feet can be quite the bone of contention. I say that *he* has the worst toes, they are long and thin, cold and wet.
'cold, wet, dead feet' is what I call them. From a jovial place of love and also: 'I love all of you except those' (as I point at the offending articles). His retort - after we've established his legs are so long, that his six foot two inch frame means his feet are too far from his heart, that's why they are dead - is that I have hammer toes.

My mum has the teeniest, tiniest size three feet, an abundance of bargain shoes - jammy or what. Me? I inherited my dad's whackers. Short and inexplicably wide big-toes, that apparently look like they've been hit with a mallet. These stubby little fellas happen to bring me joy. Out of all the body parts, I am actually quite fond of the neanderthal fuckers. A gift if you will, from my dad to me. Our daughters have one hundred precent, inherited James' finger-toes.

An unfortunate gift.

After eighteen months deep-diving my special interest on Ancestry, I traced some Maltese relatives that we did not even know we had. Six living cousins, the nephews and nieces to my dad. I'll try and keep this brief but bear with me whilst I paint a picture of the backstory without too much of a tangent.

Earlier spring 2023, my sister and I flew to Malta for a much needed chilled break and of course to meet our newly discovered family. As we were approaching the island and the pilots descent, we got chatting to our aisle neighbour about the trip. His wife was Maltese (sat further back on the plane with the teenagers) and we exchanged stories of our reason for travelling to the small Mediterranean island. Conversing about heritage and characteristics of our Maltese genes, I snort laughed as he stated that 'they are all short and have hobbit toes'… Rejoices for all five foot three inches of me and my hammer toes. My people!

Sat at a picnic bench in a pub garden in my late teens, summer sun and ice cold pints, feet free in flip flops. One of my close boy mates spotted my feet under the table and was quite literally horrified by my toes. To me they were normal. I had seen them reflected in my family and it never occurred to me that there was anything exceptionally weird about them. Ok, is this another thing I'm supposed to detest about my physical appearance, goddamn toes. Does anyone really like feet anyway? He's pointing now, not just at the width of my big toe but the chasm between it and the next one. I roll my eyes and drink my cider. This was in an era before the internet was a readily available resource from anyone's pocket. Now though, now I know that there is literally a kink for *anything*.

My brain has recently wandered to those random places of thought. There is probably someone out there that would love my toes. A rare sight, an exotic delight, maybe. Well, we are in a cost of living crisis. Where does one go to find this match and I wonder just how much they would be willing to pay for a photo. Don't judge me, times are hard and TikTok told me it's an easy side hustle.

That's as far as the musings have gone, along with the other forty-one-gajillion ideas bouncing around my grey matter. That and the fact I am not really the best at keeping up with the rigmarole of polish and pedicures, which would undoubtedly be expected if one was to profit from their pieds. One last notion sidles in. Maybe there is an even narrower niche of neanderthal wide feet, fat toes, big toe gaps and six month old nail varnish hanging on at the tip.

Different strokes for different folks.

Toe-in

the first to arrive
at many adventure
gentle taps to the
beat of the music

burrowed deep into
the hot soothing sand
the joy as they lift
and each grain
tumbles between them

skipping and jumping
down to the shoreline
lovely little toes
testing the water
preparing the rest of
my body for
what is to come

Tiptoes

sneaking into the kitchen
in the dead of night
for some delicious indulgence
illuminated face by fridge light

softly and quietly upon
the tips of my toes
into my sister's bedroom
to "borrow" her clothes

giggles in the porch
as we kick off our shoes
so not to wake the parents
as we pinball down the hall
lubricated with booze

Happy arches

can we just have one, not too much to ask
a body part of ours, yes, us women
pardoned, excused from trying to be neat
let's leave one alone, I nominate feet

pushed into shoes not fit for purpose
fish eating dry skin, anklets and toe rings
slithers of silver, do not a pretty foot make
please stop it at once, for sanity's sake

the plucking and pruning, filing of heels
trimming rogue hairs from toe knuckles
pampering pedicures, funds for the system
gel polished nails, starved of their oxygen

hoof-crushing pumps, tarsals all squeezed
soles made of card thinner than leaves
skin burnt away, wrapped in slippers of plastic
chemicals, potions, let's give them a kick

bare, naked feet, the freedom to breathe
no peril for ankles, piggies can wiggle
hot day, happy arches in solid Birkenstocks
although I do draw the line at hideous crocs

dyed hair, painted faces, satin and lace
punitive oppression, thus we're kept in our place
so give comfort to trotters, for they carry the load
laden-body so full, from the weight of this world

Grounding grass

breathe
in
hold
release
left foot, right foot
planted bare on the grass

feel the blades
between each toe
the dew
and the freshness
grounding your very soul

breathe in
hold
release

natures carpet
a comfort
restorative moments
rising from the earth
radiating up your body
to your core

breathe

Totem

do you put your
toes on the tap
in the bath
as they emerge
from the bubbles
totem poles rising
through the clouds
and yes you try
to plug the tap
with the big one

Polish

you remind me of holidays
as I prune and groom
to let you back out
into the sunshine
bright colours adorn
each nail in a declaration
of summer

Cuddle toes

two bodies
one bed
fresh, crisp duvet
as we lay
head to head
interlocking
joining
turn off the light
wrapped up
in each other
kiss goodnight
a nuzzle between
neck and nose
betwixt your
warm thighs
slip my icy toes

Ridiculous Umbilicus

Belly buttons are funny aren't they. The bringer of so much joy. Remember when you first discovered that other kids had different ones to you. Questions of 'do you have an inny or an outy?' The little crevice in the middle of your belly once sustained your life, incredible. Ok, sorry, it's not a crevice for all. Concave or convex, it attached you to your mother. Feeding you and providing you with oxygen. My first born managed to be left with an outy-inny.

Some archaic conservative types still find the navel a naughty feature that should be covered at all costs as if satan himself resides in there. Although my other half would say that poking a belly button is a definite no-go so maybe that makes it a sin. Of course that means I frequently do pop an unsuspecting digit in just to keep the magic alive. His protests include such nonsense as 'don't touch my belly button, my bum will fall off' as if it is the one thing that holds him together.

When I was in my early twenties and single, I visited my best friend at university. It was Valentines weekend and we planned a single best friends night out with a meal for two, lots of drinking and dancing. The following morning being young and impulsive we decided to go and get piercings. I already had my tongue pierced and she her belly so we went and got piercings to complete the match. I do not recommend hangover piercings. I nearly passed out. The following weekend I got together with my now husband, drunken snogs and fumbles with a raging belly button piercing is not the one. Although it did add to the hilarity of our budding relationship which has since and always will be littered with humour.

Not going to lie, I didn't realise quite how much I had to say about a belly button. Needless to say, I'm not finished. When you're pregnant there comes a point when your stomach is stretched so thin that if you do have an inny it either becomes an outy or like mine, just a flat silky piece of skin slightly darker than the rest of your abdomen. No more crevice and it was so soft, I would lovingly stroke it like a velvety puppy ear. Oh and by now that piercing is long gone. Now in my forties, I'm left with nothing more than a pin-prick hole above my navel where it was once bejewelled and every now and then if you give it a squeeze whilst in the shower, some minuscule dead cheesy skin will emerge from the dormant piercing hole.

Lint-less

sunday mornings in bed
stretched out like cats in the sunshine
lazy and docile, laughing and content
you lift your t-shirt and inspect
offering up a gift of belly button lint
a prize of fluff to collect
the ongoing in-joke between us
alas my barren button is lint-less

Champagne pools

belly button pool of champagne
carefree with wild abandon
bubbly liquid trail
an off course pathway
sparkling across hips
guiding the way for your lips
frivolous seduction
a life less serious
carving a boozy silhouette
a glorious navel puddle of post-sex sweat

Smile

my belly button
has a smile
with nipples for eyes
I know because
my daughter told me
when she was five

Butterbats

there never was a
delicate little fluttering
a gentle rhythm within
alerting me to worries
no red admiral marching
a soft beat in my belly
nor whispered swirl
of a monarch in the wind

no, for me it was a colony
restless leathery wings
took flight against my ribs
an ominous shadowy cave
cloud covered and chaotic
in the pit of my stomach
dark storm of bats rustling
trapped inside my gut
frantic mammals flying
their crescendo rising

hysteria spiralling
as if the night itself
has come alive within me

Belly rocket

there was a swing in our garden
neighbouring the apple tree
a crevice below
stamped and impacted
eight tiny feet
tattooed the earth
where grass no longer grew
four pairs of shoes
skid through the dirt

could we ever launch so high
toes not only touch sky
but a full circle turn
or sisters perched in a-frames
one in the throne
curious minds question gravity
unknown lesson afoot
mechanics and momentum
challenged an innocent game
will the speed of my rock, lift us all
my body a pendulum
wind chasing my laughs
back and forth
air now visible
between poles and ground

the best saved for last
plastic tucked just under ribs
tummy down, face to the floor
soles grapple the soil
head hanging, chains clanging
medieval drawbridge chimes
twist, turn, contort
toes teetering on tips
me versus physics…

NOW!

hands clamped tight to metal links
belly balanced on seat
lifting both legs
propelled like a rocket
wound knot, unravelling spin
air sucked from my lungs
tornado of limbs on the swing
in my garden beside apple tree
blurred vortex of motion
dizzy and free

The Largest Organ

Probably the most neglected by many, the skin. Our largest organ. I feel like we don't give our skin the credit it deserves or the attention to what an incredible part of the body it is. I have been graced with pretty youthful skin, although it has had some tougher times over the years. I had eczema as a kid. Holidays were spent avoiding the sea and sticking with the safety of the pool. The salt water didn't just taste like shit when inevitably swallowed, it would sting my face more than motor-boating a smack of jellyfish. Yes, I did just look up the collective noun for jellyfish and I'm positively delighted by my findings.

I'm allergic to plasters too. As discovered after yet another clumsy encounter around age eleven. Angry inflamed skin began to spread like wildfire from beneath the sticky Elastoplast. The school nurse tried to help by applying another, larger, more medical grade dressing in its place. Which apparently made the original raging sore go forth and multiply. I was now sporting a six inch square, furiously throbbing, friend repellent. It wasn't infectious but try telling that to a bunch of nippers yet to find their place in the social hierarchy of 'big school'. Much like when I try a mushroom to see if my palate has matured yet - no still a slug - I've made attempts over the years, to see if I've grown out of my skin's plaster aversion. Alas, no, still allergic. Literally the shittest allergy claim I have to make on medical forms ever.

Not one birth mark adorns my body. After too many criminal based TV binges, I once joked with James that if I was ever found dead (with my fingerprints and teeth removed) how would they know if it was me. I've no identifying birth marks for him to report and confirm. To which he lovingly and factually pointed out 'I think the numerous tattoos should be identifying enough'.

There was also an itchy mole removed from my back in my teens. The weirdo in me really wanted to see it afterwards. Visions of my pickled specimen, floating in its jar of formaldehyde. Maybe I could keep it, a trophy of sorts. But they wouldn't let me so much as glance in it's direction, despite it being a part of *my* body. I still haven't gotten over that injustice.

Thinking about my skin when I was younger, I can't help but remember the time when I first started shaving my legs and had zero idea of what I was actually doing. Casually submerged in the bath, armed with dad's Gillette shaving cream, no formal instructions and wielding what was essentially a very dangerous, very sharp tool. How does one know the correct pressure on their maiden voyage in body hair removal? Take aim and wing it. This technique had me slicing into the top layer of my shin as if I were peeling carrots for a Sunday roast. I wish for it to be noted, if we can practice sheathing a cucumber or banana in a rubber-johnny, maybe we could add carrots and razors to the lesson too. A flap of now dead, dormant skin was poking out from between the blades (probably only a mach two back then). Can't save that remnant for the guinea pigs. I'm grimacing just thinking about it. Not to mention the shame of my blundering attempt at becoming a young woman. The hole in my leg, pure white, now springing with dots of red, mind wandering to those minuscule red spiders, pin pricks with legs on the patio, that resembled blood splatter when squished with an index finger. Gasping quietly, I re-dipped my leg into the probably very filthy bath water, for a moment of respite. I brought my knee up again to inspect the damage and watched the clean hole refill once more with tiny red spiders, before dribbling down my leg into the waiting broth of Tesco value bubbles and slurry of shaving foam. Ouch. So much blood.

Somehow I manage to be as pale as milk in the winter months and as soon as the sun begins to shine my Maltese genes kick in. I tan instantly. Family holidays as kids I was regularly mistaken for Dutch or well, anything not English because of my golden shine. The tan, a badge of honour, the one thing I had that felt superior to my siblings. Further enhanced, stood next to my sister and her translucent limbs. What a legend, she really made me *pop*.

Until more (very) recent years, I had little knowledge of my heritage, of which, was limited to the east end of London. My mum was an only child, born and raised in Wanstead. My dad, well, this was where the heritage mystery lay. His father died when my dad and his brother were just teenagers and then their mother left them very soon after. Just upped and left for work and never came back. Obviously, I now wonder why we never talked more about the paternal side. He wasn't hiding anything from us, but there was so much we didn't know, nor did we think to ask. My sisters and I all knew that dad was born to a Maltese father and an English mother. My superb tanning skills had been passed down through my dad by his dad. We also knew that dad's surname at birth was Cutajar. He and my uncle actually changed their surname to their mother's maiden name, in a bid to better their employment prospects, in a depressingly racist Britain. I was pretty young when I was told this, yet even at my inexperienced age, it felt so unjust. To this day, it still makes me sad.

Parent-less in the late sixties he met his soon to be wife, my mum. She went to an international disco with her best friend. My cockney grandparents were racist, so I find this tidbit quite hilarious. Especially considering mum was a total goody-two-shoes (and still is). Turns out being raised by racists, makes an innocent fifteen year old, white girl, absolutely petrified of a disco room brimming with black and brown faces. Mum in fear and panic grabbed ahold of the whitest young man there and danced with him the whole time. My dad.

During winter 2021, I became completely immersed in a new special interest of tracing my family's ancestry. Certain narratives and new gems of information came to light. Dad was loving my deep-dive as much as me. I would spend hours scouring Ancestry and MyHeritage. Checking in with him after locating a new electoral role document and so on. This lead me to an extra name and when I asked dad, he was like 'oh that's my half-brother'. At thirty nine years old, I learned that my dad had another brother. This is how the search continued and resulted in the previously mentioned cousins and subsequent trip to Malta in 2023, to meet them for the first time.

Racism for me, as a white person, is a delicate subject to write about. I am acutely aware of my white privilege. The story of my parents first encounter, my dad's distinguishable Maltese features, his surname change and beige-olive to light-brown face, did however, leave me with unanswered questions. One at the top of my list was 'what race are people in Malta?'

swiftly followed by 'why are humans such arseholes?'. The hot debate of the Maltese race, wasn't what I was expecting to emerge from my Reddit rabbit hole. Therein, I discovered that the small island of Malta is a genetic recipe of many ingredients. Sicilian, Calabrians and a small sprinkle of possible Middle-Eastern seasoning. It's unsurprising given the location of Malta, that through the centuries, so many contributed to the dish that is Maltese DNA. However, as it's placed in the Mediterranean Sea and a part of Southern Europe, Maltese people are Europeans. Which on paper, makes them white, albeit on the tan-side of white and with an Arabic influenced language.

When I typed that first question into Google, I thought I'd have a cut and dry answer. What I was presented with, was so many conversations around it and many opinions. Wow, really. A conversation that has been thrashed out casually and politically for eons. Notably, as far back as the early 1900s, when a ship transporting Maltese immigrants to Australia was temporarily turned away, because politicians couldn't make their minds up whether or not they met the requirements of being white. Australian colonies had the power to discriminate using anti-immigration laws (using poll taxes). The racist *White Australia policy* forbade people of non-European ethnic origins from entering the country. British colonialism, forever and always the shameful source of my privilege.

Finally stepping foot on Malta's soil that year, was one of the best feelings I've had. A missing link had been connected and I felt an overwhelming sense of belonging. Welcomed with open arms by my cousins, all 29 percent of my Maltese ethnicity (according to the DNA spit test) beamed with pride.

Bronzed

as the seasons change
layers are removed

skin laid bare
for the sun to bronze

the heat penetrates
through my skin
to my soul within

warming and calming
tan lines carving
straps and rings

white bits, bronzed tits
balmy days, golden sun rays
joy permeates toasty skin

Goosebumps

prickles swooping
across my skin
like a Mexican wave

every hair rising
follicles responding
one by one

to a delicious touch
or a deep seated fear
becoming too much

a curious reaction
to the good
and the bad

soul igniting music
alerting my body
with a sea of tiny
bumps and shivers

Tattoos

art and memories
adorn my skin
stories immortalised
ink sketched in

"What about when you're old and saggy"

I'll have an ageing, wrinkly, artistic body

the drawings bedeck
my humble frame
no matter my age
you will find no shame

each limb painted
every decorated part
this body is mine
and I choose art

Things I wasn't allowed as a child, that I really, really wanted, a non-exhaustive list including temporary tattoos. Not least in part due to the fact they often arrived encased in another of my most coveted contraband - chewing gum.

My gum dealer was the primary school friend that was always allowed everything I wasn't. We all had one of those, right? She also had proper Nike trainers, probably funded by her lucrative career smuggling shit-listed confectionery under the pillows of all her inmates born to uptight christian parents. Though I'm not sure what the unwavering gratitude of an eight year old actually buys you. Other than a weird little shadow friend, that relentlessly knocks for you, desperate to get their mitts on some *hubba bubba* or a twenty pack of candy sticks. A sidekick that lingers worse than an eggy fart to your nan's winter curtains.

Peeling back those wrappers as the dusty mint tickles your finger tips and dances to your nostrils, sweet, sweet candy crack. You have three options;
One, pop the stick of gum straight in and of course save the paper to sniff later. I mean - for correct gum disposal later. Two, split the stick in half so it lasts longer, or to share. Three, forego the gum initially and dive right in for the tattoo. Slap that bad boy to an easily hidden body part, that is within reaching distance of your damp tongue.

I genuinely did hide packets of gum under my pillow, top bunk, wall side edge. There was nothing I loved more than silently descending the bunk ladder to ninja sneak across my bedroom à la *floor is lava*. Except it was to avoid creaky floorboards, rather than imaginary molten magma. The parkour mission was to switch on my remote-less, black and white 'portable' television, without alerting my parents of my nocturnal antics. Transfixed little criminal that I was, watching unsuitable broadcasts (from one of only four channels), satisfied and smug, whilst chomping away on a Wrigley's. One might say, infinitely less smug the time I accidentally fell asleep before re-wrapping said forbidden fruit back in it's foil. Only to wake up with it fused to my face, hair and pillow case. Or the time I looked on in horror (and a touch of morbid intrigue) at aforementioned portable, as Annie smashed Paul's ankles in with a sledge hammer. Because I hadn't grasped the concept that the watershed and maybe even my embarrassingly early bedtime, were there to protect me, a child. Not to mention, to protect my not-yet-fully-developed, very impressionable, frontal lobe from psychopathic nurses in Stephen King movies. On reflection, this may have been where my *Point Horror* book phase began.

Despite my cravings for those prohibited squares of short-term body art, I didn't get my first tough sticker until my mid-twenties. I have now lost count of how many tattoos cross my skin. There's already a mental catalogue of at least the next three or four I want to have inked, ready and waiting for some spare disposable income to swing my way.

As I got older, my mum's judgement of temporary tats had begun to rub off on me. Especially the three day old ones, unrecognisable cartoons, cracked and somewhat germy looking. It meant that my own first child was also denied the rite of passage in his early years. Don't worry, I did redeem myself once his little sister came along. You kind of learn second time around (and with some adult years under my belt), that you don't have to carry on pointless protests to harmless fun. It's not like grandmas sacred secret recipe. The absolute joy on my kids faces, as they became fully fledged members of the innocuous rebel club, was just too good not to oblige.

My sisters and I weren't allowed to join in with halloween as kids either. One of my all time favourite photos of my son and nephew, both around age three, is them dressed for halloween at nursery together. Mine was drowning in a full onesie as Sully from Monsters Inc. Velvet soft fur, paws, hood, horns and epic tail included (bloody loved that suit, it's now a family heirloom). His cousin donned a round jack-o-lantern tabard, complete with pumpkin beret atop his little pea-head. The absolute epitome of adorable, holding each other's hands whilst simultaneously channeling gangster faces that would give Tommy Shelby and clan a run for their money. Pure gold imagery, forever immortalised. Not only did I live out my childhood dreams through my offspring, I more than made up for the fun police induced FOMO throughout my twenties and thirties to heal my own inner child. Starting off strong with a superhero themed party to celebrate moving in with my boyfriend, like a proper grown-up.

In true eighties millennial style, I based my costume design very loosely on the legend that is Bananaman. By which, my super-alter-ego was Hannah Banana. Furthermore, in true undiagnosed ADHD style, I loved designing the 'HB' superhero logo, purchasing fabrics and assuming I had the skills, attention span and dopamine reserves to follow through with the sewing. After much fabric glue and felt (for the emblem), pierced finger tips with needles and copious amounts of swears, I bust out the wonder hem and iron. Yes even an iron is better than sewing. The banana yellow, top-half of my ensemble, was simply cut, cleverly folded and tied at the back like a chic boob tube. The lower, a makeshift mini in the same sunny fabric, comprised of slap-dash stitch work and a thigh split threatening a full wardrobe malfunction after one too many rums. Finishing touches included a poorly sewn, six inch wide forest green fabric belt, sat just below my navel avec piercing. A scarlet red cape (obviously) with butchered fraying edges because seamstress I am not. Attaching the cape to the boob tube with safety pins, I cleverly concealed them with improvised forest green ribbon out of fabric scraps. I want to say the chunky, dangling, cloth wristbands were banana in shape, but really, they were again, more scraps. The pièce de résistance, carefully crafted, fully measured, graphical, yellow HB affixed to a green felt octagon, stuck to a marginally larger, red felt octagon. The glorious stamp of pride. Uniting the trio of cartoon colours and quite frankly the glitter that rolled this turd of couture together.

Factory dupe revolt

north pole elves churn out
exact same dolls
carbon copies, virgin skin
production line dreary robots
the monotony of order
compliant, unquestioning

know your place
hate the body you're in

blessed be the fruit
the power hungry are watching

mother nature sighs
beautiful planet sad and boring

palette of skin tones she gave
with an abundance of hues
freckles and finger prints
art, expression, freedom to choose

paint limbs in ink
glitter cheeks sparkle blue
pierce ears, nose or helmet
should that do it for you

break free from the box
take note from birds
each rainbow rich beast
on our original earth

every fold, all the wrinkles
tell stories of worth
stripes, dots or dashes
and immortalised words

body blank canvass
awaits beautiful mess
you have one life
so live it…
NO RAGRETS

Twisty wrists

the need to prove resilience
how 'hard' you are at school
with siblings or neighbours
for no real merit at all

wrist burn challenge
twist turning the skin
shrug off pinch and burn
for a nonchalant win

quick fire reaction
slaps and thumb wars
whilst cool as a cucumber
'til skin flames raw

doodle and daydream
idle marks on your skin
sketches, reminders
of homework due in

hide holes in tights
black dots drawn on thigh
mum rants of ink poison
as if you might die

Flesh

naked touch
electric pulses
between our flesh
chest against chest
tangled legs
glistening skin
rapid breaths
salt kisses
hungry lips
push, stroke, press
flesh against flesh

Powerhouse Pair

I've definitely mentioned my height right? I'm small and I was so tiny as a child. The stunt of my height is apparently in my torso rather than my legs. I know this because I have a short body and my legs are pretty average length - tops and dresses with straps never fit right. I once stood next to my sister (same height) and my hips were higher than hers.

I was always made to feel pretty inferior, weak even, because of my height. The distain I had for sports was an extension of that really. Belief in the unsubstantiated ridicule of my useless (supposedly) little legs. One random year at around age twelve, I entered the school cross country race and somehow, weirdly was then in the school's team to run in the county competition. Speed is not something I've ever had (as in velocity, not amphetamines) but plodding along - I was evidently pretty good at. During cross country races at school my peers would pelt out of the start line in attempts to prove they were the fastest and the best. Me, I just trawled my little frame along at the same pace the entire way. Having nature to look at was the bonus I needed to keep me going. With nothing to prove to anyone, my sole aim was to finish without hyperventilating. A solid tactic for the task in hand and a pride I'd never experienced before. Go on legs!

My dabbles in running continued on and off over my adults years and always outside because otherwise what's the point. My legs saved my brain in lockdown when I fully Forrest Gump'd my way through those anxiety riddled days of despair.

After I had my first child, I was ashamed of my legs (those pesky stretch marks again!) and wore trousers all year around to hide them. I say trousers, back then they were the widest, most bonkers flares. I was a particular fan of corduroy teamed with obnoxious punk platform trainers. I was so cool. As I got older, I began to give less shits about the marks on my legs and in my thirties I decided to adorn my thighs with art. Now I confidentially wear shorts and enjoy the sun on my bare legs, the joy tattoos bring me is priceless. Also the cost per wear far outweighs any other investment.

I may not be *Johnny Sport* but the realisation that I can be active and fit without being competitive (or a dick about) was a revelation. Purchasing my first adult pair of roller skates in my twenties (which I've upgraded each decade since) was the beginning of understanding my powerhouse pair of pins. Moving my body is about delight and pleasure, not as a punishment for eating that cake. Wakeboarding, hiking, roller skating, stand up paddle boarding, total joy. These legs may not be perfect but they give me so much. I still fucking hate hills and steps though.

Sister defence

as my heart pounds
and adrenaline surges
she chases me
and my blood races
caught red handed
"borrowing" her top
we fly around the table
too scared to stop
land in the armchair
defiant and screaming
panicked breathing
not my first offence
as I lean back and kick
engaging the sister defence
cornered but smug
as I continue kicking
there's a thump I am owed
but she's not getting in

Safety lap

when they were small
they would climb
onto my lap
for cuddles or giggles
stories, a nap
these legs would bounce
with a game and a song
swishing and jumping
all day long
hold tight, fast ride
all aboard mount mummy
a kiss to the forehead
and a tickled tummy

with two full grown now
the lap can feel empty
when they are in need
I've saved hugs a plenty
I'm forever their mum
though they're bigger than me
I relish that rare moment
they sit on my knee
this place is their haven
that haven is me

Mes jambes

several drinks in at a
house party with friends
the band limber up
to serenade us with
their dulcet tones
as the acoustic strings
set in motion
the singing begins
their golden husk voices
soft notes to our ears
we smile and we sway
onto the next song
ils ont chanté en français
I throw up my arms
in a drunken stupor
declare I speak French
thump you in the leg
and laughing I shout:

J'ai mal à la jambe

Accident prone,
adrenaline junky

there wasn't a holiday that would pass
without me incurring an injury,
although there has never been
a broken bone in my body
touches wood

sprains, scrapes and scabs
screams and sobs
bashes and bruises
cradling limp limbs
plasma and platelets
red ribbon pathways
mapping a course on my skin

if there was a way
to do some damage
little me, would find it
trampolines at pontins
landing between springs
grazing layers off my legs
mum slathering wounds
in pink, stinky germolene

it did not however, stop me

from being an adrenaline junky
one life lesson transpired
from my calamitous adventures
aged ten, south of France
billy-big-balls, bravely
swung out on a rope
from a pirate ship construction
and into the sea

except I didn't make it
to the water at all
but directly below
where rough rocks
broke my fall
slicing and tearing
at my juvenile skin
red raw, glistening gashes
crude paintings on each shin

pain as the sun beat down
on fresh punctured pins
towel tents erected
for shade to no avail
sexy French doctor summoned
(that mum very much enjoyed)
nothing to do, bar lay there and wail

time to go back to base

miss all of the fun
chill, rest in the tent
pity party for one

this isn't a story purely of pain at all
for as my face sagged heavier
than a nappy on a toddler
who'd launched itself into a paddling pool
my sister volunteered as tribute
she felt bad for my predicament
leaving our other sisters to the frolics
joined me in my hour of need
ensuring I would not get bored alone

I was bloody and raw
clumsy and sad
but that day it cemented
mine was the best, the kindest sister
anyone could have had

Scandalous Ankles

Who would have thought that way back when, female ankles were the subject of such controversy. A flash of flesh from beneath the bottom hem of one's skirt - clutches pearls! A cheeky lift of the ruffles, an invitation of more to come. These days if I were to suggestively expose my ankle from under my maxi skirt you would likely be greeted with my poor neglected ankle and lower leg - I'm wearing a long skirt for a reason and it's most probably because I couldn't be arsed to shave my legs, hello hairy lil' sprouts.

When I was no more than sixteen years old, naive, young, easy pickings for weird older guys with cars. I distinctly remember once a much older bloke talking about sexy ankles (which baffled my un-diagnosed autistic brain) and he was quite insistent that I demonstrate by extending my leg and pointing my toes. Of course I obliged, poking my leg between the centre console of the car from the back seat. I don't know why they found it so amusing. Maybe it was my swift obedience, a tell tale sign of my amenability. It was not because I am so old and when I was an impressionable teenager it was the eighteenth century, no matter what my own children may believe about my age.

Ankles are quite the feat of engineering when you think about it. They hold up your entire body and connect it to your feet. Sometimes I do think my ankles are cursed by the ghost of Bambi or something because frankly they don't work particularly well and I fall over, a lot. Even now as an adult. When I look at my husband's ankles I marvel at how tiny they are, when he is far from tiny. He has sparrow ankles that seem to defy the laws of physics, holding up his tall athletic figure.

We really give them a battering too, don't we. Does anyone else manage to kick their own ankle, or is that just me? If I think about the heels I wore as a teenager trying to fit in with the crowd. The raucous raves, the aforementioned punk platform trainers, that my poor ankles have had to endure. The dizzying heights with which I have thrown myself from in blind faith that my ankles will survive the impact of landing. From the top of my bedroom wardrobe onto a severely bean-deficient bean bag below.

Most memorably in the summer of 2001, my hedonistic era of chaos, clubbing and recreational chemical consumption. A friend of a friend lived on a farm 'close by' to where the Gatecrasher's Summer Sound System festival was underway. With little cash to my name, when it was suggested we sneak in for a free rave to Pete Tong and The Chemical Brothers, who was I to decline? We all piled into a friend's car, decked out in my classic clubbing clobber. Mega wide flared trousers, tank top, Swear platform trainers and shit noughties sunglasses. We rocked up to the farm house in the middle of nowhere, spilled out into the yard to greet the others in our naughty ravers convoy.

The adrenaline positively flowing between us as we gathered to partake in some illegal shenanigans in the form of a pretty low level victim-less crime. A spot of trespassing and unauthorised access to a music event. It was hot and my feet were already heavy. There was no shade as we jovially jogged across fields in commando role-play, hand-signally 'all clear' and 'move on' to each other like ten year olds playing army. The enthusiasm began to wane as we didn't appear to be getting any closer. After what felt like several hours, we sighted a seven foot metal fence in the distance. Behind the first wired boundary was a second, creating a security watch course-way between the two. Periodically a guard on a golf buggy would trundle past and continue their journey on the outer circuit. With congratulatory smiles all round, we waited and watched for a few moments from our vantage point. Several giddy, over-lapping conversations and entry plans ensued when we looked up and saw that civvies were simply walking the perimeter until they could hop over unseen. Fuck it! Go go go. Every man for himself! Meet by the big tent. Godspeed! We all legged it to the fence, I was given a foot up and scrabbled with my thin muscle-less arms to heave myself over the top. Darted to the second fence to repeat. Tired from an afternoon scaling desolate fields but also buzzing from the rush of being caught. Seven foot high in the air, I hesitated and looked down at the dead scorched grass beneath as my friends had already begun to run off into the crowds. Some were still behind us, others had gone left to find a gap instead. Deep breaths. Fuck, security guard. I jumped down. The ground was hard and dry from all the sun and I slammed it with both feet, rolling my ankles as the impact reverberated up my body. Goddam my footwear choice. Nothing left to do but hobble-run to hide in the throng of humans. We made it. I say 'we' but it was quite some time before we all found each other. After partying all night, reaching for the lasers and hugging strangers, it was time to take the load off and sit down. Stories regaled as we lay on the scratchy grass at sunrise. Miraculously even after we split at the fence, everyone got in. We went over, some went under, a couple of my friends just walked up to a security guard and simply crossed his palm with silver to be let in. Legends.

Thankles

thanks for the twist
and the fall off the curb
just a sprain
and the holy grail
of PE exemption
as I milk this note
the apparent un-ending
ambiguous pain
and pray to
the curb gods
thou shalt never
hath PE again

Heels

the short-lived dabble in heels
a bad idea to be exact
and we just about survived
with both ankles still in tact

Sock asphyxiation

school socks in white, holes like wool lace
rolled down to the ankle, a donut in place
neon colours in pink, orange and green
pop socks and tights shimmering sheen
ankle socks sport logos, upping street cred
fluffy socks warm feet, tucked into bed
trainer socks to hide that they even exist
nora batty drooped socks, in need of a lift
over tight socks are a sadistic creation
RIP ankles, death by sock asphyxiation

Hand Span

Hands are a pretty versatile and useful body part, are they not? As humans (and also primates, pandas, koalas and apparently a waxy monkey leaf frog - who knew) we are blessed with opposable thumbs that give us limitless possibilities of uses. When you stretch your fingers out, your hand span from the tip of your thumb to the end of your pinky is the same length as your forearm... no, not your penis, (if you have one of those) but I bet many have measured against it.

Eyes are supposed to be the windows to the soul, but as I look at my hands so many memories flood back to me about what they have done, created, achieved, touched.

Holding my mum's hand as she walked at what felt like warp speed in her high heels, click-clacking on the pavement as I awkwardly jogged alongside to keep up. The circle of life as I hold my own children's hands and do the same (minus the heels). Hours upon hours playing with my sister's hair, drawing and writing throughout childhood. Lego creations, secret handshakes and rhyming, clapping games in the playground.

Fortune telling, following the life lines, premonitions of marriage, children, a house and a pool *spits* onto palm. Fond memories of dicking about in science class with friends. Hand massages on the back lab benches and secretly rolling spliffs under cover of our ring binders before nipping to the toilets under the pretence of womb troubles, to smoke it. Yes I was a liability.

Realising the joy of holding hands with friends whilst marvelling at whatever gig we are in the midst of, as the bass rumbles through our bones. A gentle squeeze of the hand in the car on long journeys. Anchoring each other's paddle boards by interlocking our fingers as we lay back, floating, drifting on the sea and soaking up the sunshine.

A random hand-holding tale of 'shit, did that just happen?'. It was circa 2004 and I was holding my boyfriend's hand, meandering up to the main arena at Bug Jam. We had embarked on the trek from our tent to the action (why is it always so far away). The rest of our friend group hollering that they would catch up with us in a bit. Dodging guy ropes and chatting away to each other, it was nice to have a moment just the two of us. Once past all the pitches we approached the track that led to the the hill. If you haven't been before, the drag racing is just the other side, everyone sits on the hill that spans the length of the strip to watch the racing.

Time for a mid-way break and probably a snog and a cigarette, we paused there a moment, stood hand in hand on the lane. When the hustle and din of a the festival seemed to have the volume muted and I realised we were both stock still and mesmerised watching a kite in the sky. The kite was attached to a lone, horizontal man atop the crest of the hill. I don't know if time actually stood still but we were transfixed, observing as the man did not move and his kite just sailed above. An other-worldly tension cloaked us, as if it was just us and him in existence. Periodically someone would walk along the hilltop passed him. Or the kite would fall to the ground again and another passerby would simply lift it to the air and carry on their course passed the man we now dubbed *dead man flying a kite*. As this scene played out before our eyes, we discussed what we should do.

'is he dead?'

'should we mount the hill and go give him a poke?'

'if he is dead, that would be a real day-ruiner'

Yes we were pretty smashed, rationale had left the building. So we just watched, rooted to the spot, the captivating contemporary dance of the kite rise, plummet and it's paralysed (possibly deceased) puppet master. Baffled by the succession of nonchalant flight enablers' actions and apathy.

Eventually, our friends caught up with us on the path. We relayed the story of events that had occurred and they joined us in viewing the surreal TV show of Dead Man Flying a Kite. After a few more kite falls and flights instigated by pedestrians on the hill, one person finally gave the mysterious, immobile, kite flyer a poke. We held our breaths and squeezed hands…

…the man got to his feet with his kite and walked off. Sounds of the fairground returned, distant bass from the big top tent and the general hubbub of thousands of people gathering in fields for shenanigans, all suddenly back in stereo. As if his steps threw us back through the quantum leap and we were both fully 'back in the room'.

Thank the lord we didn't have to touch a dead person. Oh and yes, thank fuck he wasn't actually dead. Somewhat discombobulated we followed suit, walked off holding hands, laughing and wondering if that actually did just happen.

Sure, catching and holding my babies for the first time are momentous occasions for my hand memories - but have you ever seen a dead man flying kite?

To hold

don't underestimate the wonder
of this simple touch
for it can warm your soul
when life's a little much

sometimes small, others grand
the intimate gesture
as your fingers lock together
hand inside hand

Master of arts

pen to paper
paint across walls
intricate plaiting in a sister hair train
cats cradle stringing
eye liner applying
clicking fingers
loudly clapping
frantically typing
shutter pressing
scribblings of joy and pain

Art therapy

scrambled thoughts of worry
invade my overloaded brain
expelled and pushed out
through my hands
anxiety rides the wires
sparks track each arm a branch
brush strokes across the page
a silent scream released

lost and lonely wandering
the darkest depths of my mind
an oasis amidst the chaos
desolate and stranded out at sea
an island on the horizon of relief
gold discarded knot of chains
uncoiling tendrils disentangled
slip freely from my head to fingertips

Handful

we are all older now
as we chat and we giggle
stood in the kitchen
classic chat between
a gaggle of women

mother and grown daughters
periods and boobs
the curves of our bodies
and ever changing moods

mine are pretty big
they didn't inherit from you
melons verses apples
more than a handful too

good job my man has big hands
for the challenge in mind
as mum blurts out
"more than a mouthful is a waste"

we fall about laughing
tea sprays from our mouths
then recoil, crying protests

at the sexualisation
of our own mother's breasts

Leaf and thumb

run your finger down the spine
prise it free of it's literary shrine
liberating a story and oneself
from the constructs of life and
the confinement of the shelf

hands linger on beautiful bindings
tempting you to take a dive
eagerly flipping over the book
inspect the world it pledges to provide

content by grand promises
of what you hope to find inside
fingers splay paper
leaf and thumb pages
as your mind is opened wide

It is my utmost wish that the lady from the M&S adverts could read that poem aloud. Humour me a moment and should you have the capacity in your brain (apparently some people don't even have an internal monologue!) read it again, with her voice.

Books bring me so much joy. Everything about them. Standing in a bookshop is the epitome of 'happy place' for me. Small independents are the best, not just on the morality scale but the environment and experience. Larger chain stores overwhelm me, they are usually busier, brighter and have too many options for my indecisive self. Their main focus seemingly being to sell big ticket titles from big names without any thought to the content or all the lesser knowns out there with an incredible voice or adventure to share. Give me a quiet little book nook that has painstakingly and passionately curated a wonderful collection any day.

It's comforting to be surrounded by so much thought and imagination. Eye-catching, artistic covers decorating the shelves. Picking them up one by one to digest each blurb. Is this my next read? Are you coming home with me?

The feel of a book in my hands, a solace in an otherwise shit show of a planet. Despite being a fantastic form of escapism, a moment of respite even, I was apparently drawn to characters and story lines that I had a personal affinity with. Even as far back as primary school. 'What-a-Mess' that afghan puppy was my spirit animal. 'My Naughty Little Sister' erm hello *flickering neon arrows surround my head.* 'The Worst Witch' and 'Anne of Green Gables' a catalogue of clues to my long undiagnosed Autism and ADHD.

They say (not sure who 'they' is) you can tell a lot about a person in a supermarket by what is in their basket. I think the true test is what is on their bookshelves. Recently, I've been making new friends - no mean feat - since starting to home educate our youngest. Sometimes it is difficult to determine if the mum of your child's new friend is the sort of person you should invest time into. Nothing worse than discovering they are in fact a bit racist or they vote tory, on the third play date.

Abort, abort!

Slams red button for ejector seat.

Don't worry, I'm sure there are plenty out there that have the same but opposite reservations about me - oh god, she's a liberal, feminist of the wokerati - and they mental note to avoid further contact.

I digress.

Not once, but twice over a cuppa with two different 'new friends' at my humble abode, I notice them side-eyeing my bookshelf. Both of which went on to compliment said collection. They can most definitely come again. The best thing is, that particular compilation is packed with my favourites, my special interests and undoubtedly a true summarisation of my own identity. A warm sense of pride spread through me and also a gratitude of being accepted. We have bookshelves in every room in our house. That one though, that one is all me.

My hands are forever carrying books. For some reason, I cannot migrate from my bedroom to the living room or the dining room to the garden, without a title or two in my grasp. Not forgetting umpteen other items, apparently imperative to the transition. A novel plus a non-fiction of sorts, water bottle, pen or pencil and of course the trusty notepad. This may play a part in my preference for a paperback. They are smaller, more flexible and well, there's just something wholly endearing of well read, dog-eared pages, unprotected by a hard cover. Not to mention the danger of reading a hardback in bed. The carpal tunnel threatening weight of one and the risk imposed to your face should your hands finally cave.

Earth-side

with a tribal force of nature
resemblance of galaxies
a vast universe exploding within
my mere mortal womb
transcending time and space
the essence of destiny
as life breathes life
a goddess of mythical worlds
seismic energy radiates my core
the embodiment of female power
is this actual witchcraft
the sorcery and creation
of an absolute human
grown by my own body
I reach down lay my hands on you
first to feel your tiny frame earth-side

Extroverted Sister-hands

my hands will always be here for you
dragging you from class when
you've been unfairly kept behind
by that maniac form tutor
singled out, scraping gum
from under the desks
an unwarranted punishment
for the entire class's misdemeanour

using my hands for
demonstrations
closing fingers
into an O shaped vagina
so that you can finally
try tampons

pissed, sleeping in fields
rebellious teenage exploits
rizlas, weed and tobacco
rolling limp, droopy joints

I'll hold your hand through
an emergency dental treatment
with hot swedish dentists
whilst you dribble and slur

from the injection to numb
and drain that manky abscess

during labour,
when you are scared
you cry, that you're not brave
you can't do it like me
placing my hand on yours
words of encouragement
as my body fully contracts
in sync with yours
pains of sympathy

there is nothing
I won't offer my hand to you for
from overcoming your fear of smears
to you vomiting in my cupped hands in a taxi
so you don't puke down the door

you were the shy one
and I was the gobshite
but having you in my life
gives me the strength
and the knowledge that
everything will always be alright

Sausage Fingers

It is no surprise that along with my toes, my fingers are short and rather stubby too. My sister bought me a really lovely, supposed thumb ring a few years back. Do you know where that resides now? My ring finger. It's never made it passed the tip of my thumb nail because alas piano fingers these are not.

These fingers have incessantly twiddled with my hair for as long as I can remember. Stimmy fingers - I bite the skin on the sides and constantly clean detritus from under my finger nails, in some weird repetitive ritual. Especially useful when concentrating or when riddled with nerves. Tapping on the steering wheel along to music from my meticulously created playlists.

Throughout primary and secondary school I had an innocuous bump on my middle finger where I held my pen. It would go down in the holidays and was covered in fountain pen ink term time. Comparing bumps with my mate in primary school, she showed me her massive one just below her thumb. A ganglion cyst apparently. We didn't have google then, so I'm not sure how we came to the conclusion that the only way to get rid of it, was by whacking the offending nodule with a hard-back book - her bump, not mine. I wasn't that daft.

Not only were we google-less but social media wasn't a thing either. Our status updates and tweets consisted of writing on each other's backs with our index finger until the friend guessed what we'd written. Painstakingly drawing out letters, giggling and rubbing the "canvas" as if to erase the previous message before starting again.

It may be apparent that I have touch of the potty mouth. I've never put much onus on swear words. They're just words and despite swallowing a dictionary for breakfast as kid, I will always revert to some of my simple favourites. Also a fan of flicking the V's between friends in an endearing way. One Christmas in my early twenties a giant box of Cadbury's chocolate fingers ended up in my possession. After several festive drinks (and whatever else) the metre long box became a prop in our tom-foolery (fuck-wittery, if you will) when it was proclaimed *the biggest box of fuck-yous ever.*

When you give birth (as I have done three times now) the memories come back in intermittent flashes. So much time is spent focussing on the job in hand and I imagine eyes are shut for a majority of the event, mine certainly were. It's like an internal camera switched on and caught micro moments and stored those in my brain. My youngest came into this world in the birth pool at home and as I opened my eyes to catch her head, the umbilical cord was wrapped around her neck. Instinctively my fingers gently prised the loop over her. Was I imagining it or was there still cord there? As my mind was processing this, James' finger appeared and repeated the motion. Twice! Two times that cord was tangled. Hurrah for life-saving speedy fingers.

Feeding the ducks

throwing in bread at the side of the lake
arms raised, crusts between fingers
excitement and bustle children flanking each side
my brain starts to linger

the boisterous sounds echo across the water
sun beating down toes poised just at the border

time seems to have frozen
the movement though swift plays out in slow motion
my entire body followed my hand
which followed the bread
that I forgot to let go and threw myself in instead

not one person has noticed my rookie mistake
submerged in the water
panic cries, muscles ache
fingers clutching the grass and the weeds
on the side of this lake

it felt like a lifetime
probably mere minutes
rescued by dad
laughing off near death
to lift all our spirits

a squish and a squelch
each footstep I took
trudging back to the car
soaked through denim
a curious look

thank god for sisters
the same size as me
clothes swap tag team
to gloss over the chaos
and grab an ice-cream

Hand-picked

rows and rows
of bountiful treasure
a blanket of berries
calling to be touched
crouching pudgy knees
foraging through leaves
our fingers twists stalks
fruit as fresh and plump
as our puerile cheeks
two for the punnet
and one for my tongue
sweet flesh devoured
the taste of summer sun

Mood

the kudos and accolade
of one tiny ring
cheap and garish
my very favourite thing
a child who struggled
to name any feeling
now I could look
at the coloured auras
my finger was manifesting

Sucker

'Suck thumb, dirty bum' the taunt of shame croaked at me by my great nan. My one comfort. We enter the dingy east London flats with the unmistakable pungent whiffs of lead and piss in the echoey corridors, assaulting my little button nose. Preamble to the weirdness of this obligatory duty. One must appease the ancient relic, highest but most fragile bag of bones and skin atop our family tree. Every time it's the same, thick cloying air, knitted sausage dog draft-excluder barricading the slither of hope of some oxygen. She stares from the comfort of her granny chair, dentures forgotten, alabaster face, gummy grin 'take that out, you don't know where it's been' My response, a gentle wet pop from my mouth, beloved thumb begrudgingly removed.

The worst of it is, I know the next task beset to me, is to give this slightly dribbling, victorian cockney a kiss. It's what happened in the eighties. Requirement not choice. Great grandkids *must* hug and kiss wrinkly relatives as a way of formal greeting or to take one's leave. Can't be rude to the queen. 'suck thumb, dirty bum' I never understood what she meant due to being a very small child. It remained filed in the box of confusion in my brain, along with 'you'll get piles' that time my nan saw me sat on a cold doorstep, outside my friend's house. Piles of what? Paper? Nan be crazy.

Before you know it, you're twenty eight years old in the pharmacy bulk buying threadworm tablets, because the fruit of your loins was up all night, with an itchy arse. Petrol bomb the bedding and move house. The four of us medicated with the de-wormer like tabby cats - just to be on the safe side. Only for the first born to have an allergic reaction to the fucking tablet! Appearing in the morning, face like Professor Klump and fear of death in his eyes. It had, as yet, not been deduced that I'd basically poisoned my son (sorry, I'm feeling dramatic). Frantic phone calls and a trip to hospital. Nine hours quarantined for 'maybe mumps' when all he needed was a couple of spoons of Piriton. To say I had some thought space to wander would be an understatement. Dear friends this is when the moment of clarity rang.
'suck thumb dirty bum' roughly translated over the generations, to me now, nagging my kids.
'Wash your hands' 'Stop biting your nails, it's unhygienic' Because… bum worms.

May I take this moment to whole-heartedly apologise, if you've suddenly become afflicted with a *psychosomatic scratch* - exceptional band name material.
I shall redeem myself forthwith. Please join me on a

pilgrimage of all the moments, places and things for fingers and thumbs, better than bum worms...

Finger pilgrimage

fingers knotting friendship bracelets
held in place by cassette tape cases
peeling backs from album stickers
align right angles to stick in pages
pushing doorbells for friends to play
press record top forty hits
pause a beat skip talking bits
shushing mimes at sisters
lest their voice accidentally check the mic
twisting gum from between lips
shredding bark from dried out sticks
releasing bats from nostril caves
discarded wipes and flippant flicks
tapping tunes on desks
dancing digits stride piano keys
arise josh baskin, boy in man skin
reciting rap to every word
not knowing what a triscuit is
clicking fingers louder still
do mumbled lyrics snaps conceal
brush crumbs of powder onto gums
as friends turn tables scratch vinyl disks
poked in ears to plug vibrating bass
smearing tired all-nighter face
tracing jaw lines

tickling pits and knees
rub circle rhythms on shiny pearl
like juicy sugar plum
pressed against lips with winks
silenced knowing secrets kept
freeing zips of bulging groins
treasured nips teased by thirsty thumb
picking salty crisps from teeth
dipped in pools of hot candle wax
scratching scalp hat-hair released from cap
signalled swears behind siblings back
smooth warm amber over rocks
measured double finger deep

late night guiding ink in words
glowing screen in palm
tired brain misplaced wanton verbs
cramping claws complete

it's two am ten digits cry

click

the

lamp

now sleep

Cool AF

marlborough menthol held
aloft between fingers
puffing like a lady muck

dear little fifteen year old me
doesn't care for your disdain
frankly this is cool as fuck

smoking is not cool kids... it was the 90s ok! Besides it really did look cool in the movies

Guard dropped

the unwritten rule of
any long term relationship
up the stairs one by one
or unawares in the kitchen
head down in the washing machine
is it a finger, is it a thumb
bend over unguarded
you will get a poke in the bum

Exploration

discovering the truth of my body
with my own fingertips

an adventure below borders
wandering touch slips

sweet juicy fruit
lightening tremor

at the end of these digits
bewitching power

sparks of delight
jump across prickled skin

a hunger and heat
rumbles deep within

frantic breaths
each rhythmic circle

sweet satiated release
as knees buckle

Mud Manicure

the joy a muddy set of digits brings
from a solid day bumbling about the garden
paint splattered fingers from art or decorating
accidentally adorning my face with war paint
as I brush my hair from my eyes

Hair is Everything

The 'pencil' scene from one of my very favourite shows, which honestly I'm not going to write because I'm scared of lawyers and copyright and god forbid I upset the legend that is Phoebe. Is that enough clues? If you know what I'm talking about, we can be friends.

Back to the hair, it isn't actually everything and I've learnt a lot about that over the years. Not least in part because of my daughter's alopecia, which I knew nothing about before she was diagnosed but now I can wax lyrical for quite some time over it. I have this innate ability to research like Meredith and Cristina in the face of a medical mystery. If I don't know about a subject and it affects my life or someone very dear to me, then I hit the books, google and research articles. It's one of my many Autistic & ADHD traits that I really quite like.

When her hair first started to fall out she was bedecked with the largest collection of hats until eventually there were more patches than hair, so we shaved it all off and she raised money for Alopecia UK in the process. She absolutely rocked her buzz cut and the unique patterns of her scalp. I offered up my barnet in solidarity when my husband interjected and took his seat on the throne instead. She had the most fun shaving his into a Mohawk before going for the full nut cut. In a surreal turn of events we all ended up on the local ITV news as they talked about her fundraising and the blog I helped her write to share her experience for other young children with the same condition.

Hair is how we express our identity of which I have had many throughout my life. A lost and confused child, I never really knew who I was or where I fit in but I tried my damned hardest. Some styles I chose for myself and others just because that's what everyone else was doing. My undercut in the early nineties was a fave. Whilst all my girl friends had long locks, there I was with my undercut and curtain bangs. Around the age of nine or ten, I was mistaken as a boy with my gelled spiky hair. My oldest sister was taking me to the senior school fete when one of her classmates asked 'is this your little brother?'. I'm not sure why, but back then I was deeply offended, I mean, a purple shell suit and short hair was not the uniform of a single gender, *I am clearly a girl* or so I thought. Also boys are smelly, so there. I ran home and put on some quality green eyeshadow and pink lipstick to return to the day's frivolity looking like a four-foot Boy George in his *I wasn't expecting visitors* lounge wear.

It's not surprising that I wanted all my hair cut off as a child, I'll never forget the tension pull of my mum plaiting it for school. Poor woman did have four daughters to get through and I could not sit still for mine, nor did I sit quietly about it. Repeated threats of 'Sit still or I'll cut it all off!' finally galvanised in a series of chops by my own request.

It's hard to recollect the exact moment in time when I went from a weird, quirky child to someone that started worrying about body hair. I must have spent something like eleven years not even contemplating that the hair sprouting from my limbs was anything but normal. One PE lesson in year seven, a class mate was giggling about the teacher's hairy knees showing in her gym shorts. Baffled, I was truly baffled. What do you mean? Doesn't everyone have hair on their knees?

Once puberty hit, the need to fit in, blend and be liked by my peers was strong. My hair had grown out and I started to dabble with colour - an impulsive activity that still plagues me in my early forties. Wash-in-wash-out sachets, a gateway to stronger more permanent chemicals. First up were the reds, teamed with a striking blue nail polish at thirteen and being told by nan that I looked like a 'cheap tart'. Ammunition for the determination to rebel with my fashion sense as much as humanly possible, albeit limited to what I could stuff in my pockets (alongside a heather shimmer lippy, a bottle of *So* perfume and a razor for the pubes I'd yet to grow) without being caught at the local pharmacy.

13 reasons

short hair is not just for boys
long hair will get caught in your armour
Joan of Arc was wise

hairdryers are fucking loud
and mangle your long hair
if it so happens to dangle and
suck into the rear *(it has happened)*

you can dye it more
and not worry about the damage
just choppity chop it off

short hair doesn't get in the way
when you go down

a zombie can't catch you
by your locks as you run away
ask Carol, she knows

you don't have to plan
your hair wash days

no need to try and perfect
the messy bun, which does in fact

take longer to get right than
just washing it in the first place

you won't accidentally burn
your hair on candles
when casting witchy spells
on your enemies

that selfie you took
with a famous on a windy day
wouldn't have been ruined
by your hair across your face
(true story)

infinitely less knottage

considerably less sweat
during a heatwave

gender is a social construct
boys already have more pockets
have short hair if you want to

it's French!

Sex hair

a night spent in bed
the beast with two backs
acrobatic antics
sweaty fun in the sack

morning look in the mirror
smiling at my reflection
a sex badge of honour
hair in every direction

laughing I turn to you
'I look like a Cockatiel'
grinning right back you reply
'like you've had a cock or two'

Death by tweezers

R.I.P to the brows of the nineties
plucked to death by tweezers
I was too scared of pain to use them
so secretly used a razor
I shaved away the under brow
in a need to have them thinner
thank the lord it meant they grew
as I was just a mere beginner
by the time big brows came back on top
my un-plucked-arches were winner

Watching paint dry

eagerly awaiting that first pube
checking again
still nothing
like watching paint dry

finally they begin to emerge
as you reach for your pink Bic
and lop'em off anyway

Shower massacre

have you ever eaten
too much beetroot
forgotten about it
until you flush the loo
and assume
you are about to die
as a bright red toilet bowl
stares back at you

a similar event
eyes shut in the shower
after a night on the dance floor
and after party too
washing away
the fag smell
lathered in shampoo

I look down at my
wet naked body and blink
thoughts of head lacerations
flash through my mind
as I remember…

I'd dyed my hair pink

Contradiction

one single hair
and the pain
it can bestow
caught in a strap
or the hinge
of your glasses

yet all pulled at once
into a satisfying knot
brushed out
scalp scratched
wrapped around fingers
a fistful in passion
a cheeky tug

Magic brush

rhythmic motions
from crown to nape
each bristle a tiny magic wand
as it sweeps through every strand
skimming down the mane
brushing in love
and pushing out pain

for happy days
for cuddle days
for sad days
and overwhelmed days
for loving days
and cherished days

rhythmic motions
from crown to nape
each bristle a tiny magic wand
as it sweeps through every strand
skimming down the mane
brushing in love
and pushing out pain

Fringe Regret

how many times
can you see in your mind
the new do
a face frame
of hair for you

yes a fringe
to slice across your brow
reach for the scissors
blades poised
no stopping you now

Wind whipped

making a figure of eight with your friend
holding each others crossed hands
face to face, toe to toe,
spinning as fast as you can
here for the dizzy, don't let go
heads thrown back, eyes to the sky
the wind whips through your hair

is this what it feels like to fly?

human crash test dummy
for the neighbour's handmade
rickety bike trailer, because,
well you're the smallest and the lightest
full teenage-boy-speed across the bridleways
no helmet, white knuckles, bugs in your teeth
and the wind whipping your hair

is this what it feels like to fly?

double up for bike-backies
arms wrapped around their waist
grabbing hold of jackets
like your life depends on it
which it really does

bike tyres striking curbs, rocks,
bumps reverberating through your arse
free wheeling down the hills
and wind whipping at your hair

is this what it feels like to fly?

first time on your boyfriend's
crappy 50cc moped
trespassing over tractor routes
revving through fields of wheat
stand up steering, hollers of joy
clothes flapping at your flesh
wind whipping hair free of your face

is this what it feels like to fly?

strapped in, locked and loaded
overhead bars between you and concrete
cranked to the heavens, clunk, clunk, clunk
humans like ants on the ground
questioning the two mitsubishis
you swallowed in the queue
the world's first vertical drop rollercoaster
wind whipped hair shooting for the sky

is this what it feels like to die?

Resting Bitch Face

I've lost count of the amount of times people have asked me if I am in a mood because I have forgotten to engage my brain with communicating to my face that I am absolutely fine. Being Autistic it can be a conscious decision I actually have to make and sometimes I'm too tired or distracted to remember.

The best tool for scaring my teenager's friends into thinking I'm a scary mum, when I'm actually far from it, which of course they realise once they get to know me. Dude, this is just my face.

That said, I do quite like my face. It's alright. As a child I don't remember giving my face much thought for a really long time. Then of course you learn what the *normies* expect of your visage and before I knew it I was slapping on the veritable mask subconsciously, for a real long time. I would say my appearance was somewhat comparable to that of the classic *ugly duckling*. I changed schools in my very early teens (standard un-diagnosed neurodivergent teenager practice). When I eventually began to hang out with my old school friends again, there was a touch of a glow up. Which evidently got me noticed by the boys and I was quids-in with the lusty, grope-y, youth.

Pre-glow-up, I had gnarly teeth because my milk teeth fell out and didn't grow back for about a year, leaving behind a huge gap between my front gnashers. Somehow I avoided a brace as when my adult teeth grew they naturally pushed everything back into place where they should be. Black eye-liner had become an extension of my skin, applied religiously every day.

It's funny that even though my own face never really offended me personally, I never really associated myself as someone who was *pretty*. Even now, I'm like, my face is *ok*. I realise it's weird to feel this way about my own reflection as we (as in women) are supposed to look in the mirror and pick all the faults possible. Yes I am getting a little wrinkled and writing books doesn't give me enough disposable income for botox (although I have dabbled in the past). If we focus on my actual features, rather than wear and tear. My green eyes… the pupils are haloed by amber like a magical abyss bursting through a planet dense with lush, tropical rainforests for continents. Green just so happens to be my favourite colour. Teeth are straight enough (they'll do). Nose is *normal*, with a hint of those Maltese genes, a smidge wide, most definitely chubby. This nez is blessed with exceptionally large, round nostrils and the capability to spontaneously flex to beat of the bass - just because I can. It's a good nose and I'm keeping it.

On the flip side of the RBF, when I am deliriously happy, it spreads animatedly through each feature between my forehead and chin, right through to my limbs. Toothy grins from ear to ear, double chins of joy and happy dances. Pure and unadulterated expression. This is how I like to think of my boat-race. After a recent photoshoot with a very good photography friend, I chose a favourite image and this was the exact vibe I was drawn towards. I realised that this is the *me* I want people to know the most. My friend said 'I always think of you laughing when I see your face in my mind'. There's an honest, authenticity to it. Whereas the serious, posed photos just feel fake to me. Not to mention, with my *resting bitch face*, it just doesn't work.

Contrasting visage

a look that exudes maturity when just a teen
passing for the legal age to purchase cigarettes
a contradictory metamorphosis into adulthood
gasps from strangers that learn my real age
accusations of being an actual vampire
that bathes in the blood of virgins

Friend stamps

a grid of joy
four images of our faces
squished in close up
the intimate sequence
that a photo booth brings
adolescent antics
the freedom of a bus ride
escape the scrutiny of parents
through dank concrete districts
cinema trips and shopping days
the package complete
with a souvenir to cut and divide
to share and remember
packed into a passport photo booth
a portal of our youth
sunrise stop at the services
post clubbing all-nighter
accidentally raving to the sound
of an industrial cleaner
rotating a monotonous beat
as it buffs at the floor
in our own little world
off our tits laughing
hold tight for each click
one face, two face, three face, four

Mirror, mirror

we have been awake for hours
deep and meaningful
ecstasy fuelled conversation
as we get lost in the mirror
the size of our pupils
make-up smudged in
sweat tracks across cheeks
anthropology, philosophy
observations and consultations
forgetting our words mid sentence
as we stare down each of
our gurning reflections

Smurf

have you ever just let your child go wild
with a pot of snazaroo
but all you have is what you bought
in a world book day panic
he wanted to be sonic
black, white and blue

you're tired, sleep deprived
possibly hungover too
eyes dry, sand paper tongue
a sit down activity is in need
so you let his little sister
loose with a sponge

wet slaps of paint
her pudgy little fingers
criss cross your cheeks
head, neck and nose, excitedly slathering
never-ending inner mum guilt
the joy on her face, pulls at your heart
matching sky blue mini-me
a true smurf of art

Third time's a charm

imagine sculpting for the first time
into this clay you work your everything
care, attention, sweat and moulding

this piece is going to be an original
with a touch of your personality
a marked semblance of familiarity

the longest most gruelling project
fusing features a unique design
the parts of you are going to shine

delicately placing my art in the kiln
excited to unveil unrivalled creativity
for the bloody thing to look nothing like me

that is what growing an entire human
regrettably turns out to be, rather,
an exact, somewhat mini replica of their father

the traitorous alien, baked in this fleshy oven
couldn't even have the decency or grace
to emerge from my vagina with a hint of my face

not once, but twice, this repeated occurrence

the effort and sacrifice, you're kind of sad
when the second carving mirrors her dad

seventeen years later from the first offence
another surprise creation on her way
bear down, birth out, this metaphorical clay

to my breast, the tiniest creature
breathe in that intoxicating new baby smell
chubby little nose, round eyes, tears begin to well

finally my genes have chosen to emerge
familiar features in the crook of my arm
for art is a process and third time's a charm

let it be known, I adore the faces of all my children, but it does seem a bit unfair that after the human grower does all the hard work, their genes don't seem to be as prominent. I am also aware that there is an evolutionary theory, that the resemblance helps the father recognise the fruit of their loins. Thankfully James didn't eat our Mila cub, like a lion may have.

Bare faced liar

the brazen audacity of youth
invincible, unstoppable
and yes a bit selfish

but fuck me, life is for living
and maybe Dave and Karen
are selfish in a way

there's no chance I'm going
to be able to *officially*
book the holiday days

those two beat me to it but
there's a very important festival
in France, I must attend

the hustle of *lining one up*
that B in GCSE drama
standing me in good stead

cough

               cough

                              cough

clutches head

deliberately wearing less make-up
sat at work feigning sickness
a ploy for all to bear witness

'go home' they declare
don't spread your germs here
home to my packed bag of festival gear

a glorious long weekend ahead
raving in the fort ruins at St Malo
pre-social media days, no-one will know

singing in the car with your best friend
on the way to Portsmouth for the ferry
rumbles of lies and excitement deep in the belly

white vans, a truck full of chickens
pass by commuters sat forlorn in their cars
'if that truck was behind us,
we'd have a thousand smelly cocks up the arse'

jokes and escapades
beach trips, mosh pits
laughter for days

unwashed camping hair
shitty port-a-loos and sisterhood

wild wees in the woods

freedom, lost inhibitions
those highs us young adults crave
wrapped up, presented, in a form of a rave

alas, I was careless
maybe karma was at play
for the first night I *was* sick
bed early, dozed listening
to my friends round the fire pit
tent left open to still feel a part of it

returning to work the next week
a minor scupper to my carefully crafted plan
no less than ten mosquito bites on my face
and a fucking sun tan

Mouth

Each time I start a chapter there are one of two ways I begin. The first, a readily reserved catchy title or words that tickle my brain just so. Alternatively, when the diction isn't, err, dic-ing, I simply write the body part, until my waffle conjures the former. So, I wrote *Mouth*. With an uncanny witchy tendency, it instantly summoned Corey Feldman to the forefront of my very photographic brain. Not him currently, but from 1985 as Mouth in the absolute classic that is The Goonies.

Is it any wonder that I have an affinity with this character, given that as a child, I too, was consistently admonished for talking too much. Well to be perfectly honest, it's a personality trait that remains resolutely into my forties. Not only do I talk (apparently) too much, but I also cannot keep quiet when I think there's an injustice at play or if someone has unexpectedly pressed my *special interest* button. Lord-a-mercy for anyone who vocalises an entirely incorrect statement linked to one of those interests.

Suffice to say, my mouth also got me into quite a bit of trouble. The injustice warrior in me could not hold back. From primary school to adult jobs, crusades included standing up to teacher and colleague bullies alike. Not for myself silly, for other people, the disabled or marginalised peers, the underdogs or the younger employees. There's nothing that sets my mouth 'on one' more than a person using their elevated role to beat someone down with. Unwritten or widely noted hierarchies hold zero weight for me. You want my respect, then respect me and above all, respect those at a disadvantage to you. Respect is earned. That convoluted, triple barrelled, middle management job title on your email signature, does not automatically bestow a free hall pass directly to the door of character nobility. The same goes for 'elders'.

If one should find oneself decorated with the medals of privilege, enfranchised by the social constructs of hierarchy… please don't be a dick.

Battle cries

whilst I have breath
in my lungs
I will cry

hail to the rooftops
until the tiles shake
unfairness heard

scream through cities
shoulder to shoulder
kindred warriors

levy my privilege
for all wrongly hurt
holler support

every grievance
mark my vote
noted and fought

tell family and friends
there's work ahead
the world can do better

rise up and roar

against violence
oppression and rape

educate myself
homophobia and racism
unlearn what was told

nurture this planet
raise a new generation
on humanity's side

yell at the universe
drown out hate
for action is hope

down family lines
my part in history
will bear no regret

whilst I have breath
in my lungs
I will cry

howl to the moon
for the humans I made
and those never met

Blessed be the safe foods

thank you for the gift of safe foods
grant me the strength to fry an egg
whilst resisting the thoughts
of it being too eggy on the third bite
and the wisdom to smash the avo onto toast
before it's sat in the fridge drawer
sad and overripe

help me to remember
that macaroni cheese from a can
is the work of pure evil
but freshly made, super cheesy
bubbling and oven baked can cure all
especially with a side of garlic bread
all hail the double-carb

patience may be a virtue
but if all else fails
there is always the holy hot bagel
with butter and marmite
may the crisp stash be plentiful
halloumi squeak and cucumber crunch

in noodles we trust, ramen

Chase

the thrill of it
juvenile legs dart from one end to the other
a game of tag but with added peril
zigzagging the playground
in a bid to outrun and outsmart
the wandering grabby mitts
of kiss thirsty boys

Word Vomit

I talk too much apparently
always chastised by teachers
for chatting relentlessly
the spaghetti junction
that circulates my brain
has to go somewhere
forever word vomiting
to an unsuspecting ear
talked my friend to sleep
with verbal diarrhoea

to be fair
it was *her* personal request
she needed to sleep
a post-partying rest
to get up for work
too scared to miss out
it was my duty
taken very seriously
as the dawn was calling
our gang still living-room-raving

we would lie together
upstairs on the bed
and she instructed me

to just keep talking
anything from my head
but not to stop
until she was content
in the land of nod

quite the skill
an exceptionally fond memory
of friendship
of connection
wistfully reminiscing
those moments of carefree
low responsibility
time-rich days.

fuck
when did we get so old
that we don't have time
to talk each other to sleep anymore

we would laugh about
growing old together
what we would look like
in our care home
the trouble we would cause
hairy mole on her chin
me with my jowls

silver haired
rebellious little grannies

I read a book this year
the two protagonists
conversed by pen
unfaltering exchanges in notes
my middle-aged heart
was warm and fuzzy
transported to the days
when she went to university

letters, cards, emails
extensively written
back and forth
coloured inks and doodles
like the evidently geriatric woman
I now am
I wished and I missed
the pre-social media
the pre-smart-phone days

digging out
a lined a4 pad and pen
I started to scribble down
a good old-fashioned
ink and paper letter to my mate
posted in the snail mail

oh the joy
the writing
the sending
the receiving
two days later
a giddy WhatsApp note
when it was poked
through her letterbox
my vomit of words
on the matt by her door

let's just pretend that
she didn't just ping me
her gratitude from an iPhone

turns out
having grown-up jobs
a mortgage, kids
adult expectations
really fucks with
your penpal obligations

Mouthgasms

ice poles after water fights
those paper-cut-esque slices
from their plastic edges
on corners of your mouth
not so much

sunday afternoons
sat on the floor
tray of plates, cutlery and butter
toasting bread on a skewer
glowing coal embers
in the open fire
like a proper victorian
whilst watch the borrowers

jolly ranchers
tangfastic cherries
dip dabs, flying saucers
sherbet lollies
popping candy
icepops of shandy

crunchy crisps
full of flavour
and the density just so

round discos
sharp vinegar dusted
rib'n'saucy niknaks
pickled onion monster munch

Sabotaged By My Baby Box

Embarking on this chapter as I sit on my patio, feet up, massive apple-catcher-pants on, surrounded by a plethora of post-surgery paraphernalia, peppermint tea, books to stave off the boredom, love heart sweets - which I am reliably informed, are the secret to alleviating gas that feels like golf balls ricocheting through your intestines - the time was now, time to celebrate what was once my uterus.

There was a period of time when I couldn't muster any enthusiasm for the book. A so-called fiesta of fun and frolics inspired and born from my own body parts, it felt like a lie, a deception, as mine was betraying and torturing my very existence. My mind and mojo had been flushed away with each cycle and tsunami of blood.

It's hard to think positive thoughts as you manically mop up a crime scene of claret in the disabled toilet of the Natural History Museum. Wads of tissue, wiping away the hourly torrent of crimson between my thighs. The shame as I realised the toilet was now blocked and there were people the other side of the door waiting to access the loo. Thank the old gods and the new, as I gingerly unlocked and peered out with my guilt leaden eyes, I saw a janitor armed with sprays and reems of bum-exfoliating toilet paper. Anxiously I explained the predicament of the porcelain massacre scene behind me.

'it's blocked…'

Hesitating, not wanting him to think I've taken a massive shit.

'… it's blood, I don't want to scare or worry anyone'. Then I run off with my daughter in tow to find some fossils, until the chaos ensues and repeats. A snapshot into life with uterine fibroids, ovarian cysts and adenomyosis. Not just inconvenient on day trips to London but also sapping every ounce of energy from my very bones. The laughter and joy was literally leeching from my womb.

Light is now beginning to appear at the end of this tunnel, the tunnel of my vagina. This troublesome body part has been forcibly evicted. My pelvis the host to a fleshy nest, giver of life, is now raw, bruised and empty. My bladder and bowels tender and confused as they shift to fill the void. Once the morphine and post-surgery trauma began to evaporate from my bed of rest, I grabbed my notebook and pen. Reminiscing in scrawls, annotations of what this pear shaped piece of anatomy meant to me, what she brought me, the taboo, the politics, the humans she grew. She had a good innings. Farewell fallopians, see you later ovulator and thank you for your service.

The youngest of four daughters to my baby obsessed mum, I always knew that one day it would be my turn. Mum had books and stories on pregnancy and birth. Dorling Kindersely editions with intricate images a plenty. My personal favourite, the twins in utero. She didn't particularly like animals, unless of course it was a baby animal, lambs, chicks, any newborn creature. Which is a good job really, especially considering the time I coerced my sister into pairing up one of our female hamsters with the male hamster we were pet sitting for a friend. The two of us facilitated the rodent date on the worktop of our utility room. We decided not to use our own hamsters, but the hamster of another sister (who was blissfully unaware of our intentions). That was until Tiny started acting weird, a little aggressive towards hands in her cage and spending hours filling her cheeks with bedding from the little house and transporting it through the tunnel into the secondary cage, to apparently create a nest in the corner of the tray. Maybe she was poorly, hamster flu? Talks of vets and pondering of what could possibly be wrong with her ensued.

One morning, I was home sick from school and decided to peer under said nest of shredded paper. There I spotted a cluster of pink jelly babies. Placing the nest back, I congratulated the new mum and began to pace, deliberating the consequences of my actions and the bollocking I was going to get when mum came home at lunchtime.

'Mum, what would you do if Tiny had babies?'

'Well she wouldn't as we only have girl hamsters'

'Yeah, but what would you do?'

'It's not possible though… unless, unless…'

By this point it is definitely written across my face.

'…unless someone put her with Choccie… you didn't… did you?'

I hold my breath and nod.

Lunch abandoned, she rushes straight to the utility and I follow, guilty as charged, bracing for impact.

Mum melts the very second she sees them, despite their hairless, eyes-closed impersonation of the blush plastic pigs we used to have for our toy farm.

The miracle of life exonerating me from my misdemeanour.

Watching them grow was pretty cool. Their little characters, their fur finally growing. Some had his markings, brown chocolate splodges, others more like her. A beautiful lesson in procreation, parenthood and what happens when you put two adolescent mammals together without adult supervision. A lesson, I did not heed and on reflection, probably shouldn't have been the start and end of my sex education at home. No more than around four years later, aged sixteen, I found myself with a tiny lodger of my own, nestled inside my womb.

Unspoken

the first time I saw a tampon
mum was showering
I was no older than five
she knew I had entered
although I couldn't tell you why
probably as I sensed she had
just one moment to herself
opened the door and snuck inside

'won't be long, I'll be out soon'
or words to that effect
when I spotted a little something
a small unknown object
my little mind must inspect

despite having no idea
what this small packaged thing is
I felt naughty and sneaky perched
with my treasure upon toilet lid
crinkles and whispers at finger tips
sounds disguised with the shower's
persistent splashes and drips
my palm pumping shame
plastic wrapped secret stories forbidden

questions and answers left hanging
unspoken

Juxtapostion

teenage pregnancy bump
ungodly
tainted
unmarried mother
definitely not an immaculate conception
hand-me-down maternity wear
charitable gifts
from friends at my parents church
good christian clothes
shrouding my sin heavy belly
truly I was grateful I had nothing else
but what a sight to behold
dowdy draped frumpy bump
to a baby-faced hussy

Older brother

how would you like to have
a brother or a sister
I'd really like an older brother
little sister is best I can do
a disappointment
I hope is not akin
to the nicks trainers
I had to endure
when I really wanted
the bloody nikes
but we were too poor

Russian dolls

I recently learned that
when I was in the confines
of my mothers womb
cells dividing and multiplying
transforming alien like creature
to mini human
that inside my freshly grown ovaries
whilst inside my mum were all the eggs
this foetus would carry
mothers of daughters
a blood line of russian dolls
my mother harbouring me and mine
the visions conjured
of the old lady who swallowed a spider
or an april fool present
a box inside a box inside a box
digital art hiding secret worlds
in an eyeball of a portrait
pinch and zoom
now my mind is lost
wandering a hall of mirrors
a parallel dimension
disturbed and discombobulated
in this tangled though tangent
eggs within a foetus within a womb

Who says my meme addiction isn't educational. Because that's how I discovered this nugget of information. Don't worry, I did of course fact-check my findings *inserts blue tick*. As with many of my deep dives for information, down a rabbit hole I fell.

For instance did you know that an embryo is named as such only until eight weeks and then it is a foetus. Which was a bit annoying because I was going to use the word embryo when I wrote that poem. The foetus doesn't have fully developed ovaries until about twenty weeks - ergo not an embryo - so I had to re-use the word foetus. Americans spell it *fetus*. It is not technically a baby until birth (take note US and Tories).

Ovarian follicles begin to form in utero at twelve weeks and the hamburger - labia buns and clitoris burger - around thirteen weeks. If you ever frequented pregnancy forums, the ultrasound hack for establishing the sex was hamburger or hot dog. What completely blew my mind is at twenty weeks her reproductive system is complete, including several millions of eggs. This brain boggling amount drops at birth to just one or two million, then ten thousand less each month until she reaches puberty. We never grow new eggs. In contrast boys don't produce any sperm until they actually hit puberty.

Politicians like to get hung up on establishing sex and gender as binary, black and white, that anything converging from their idea of normal is 'unnatural'.

It is maddening when 1.7% of the world population are intersex. That's *one hundred and thirty six million* people. A natural human occurrence that isn't as rare as you think. Statistically comparable to those born with red hair. Even my first pet dog had a penis and wait for it… ovaries! An interesting revelation when the vet thought he was going in to oust the pup's retained testes. We did not give a shit, he was still Rocco. Loyal, loving, velvet soft ears and could clear a room in seconds with his anxiety farts. He couldn't speak human, so we never got to ask him what his preferred pronouns were. We speak human though, you and I, and politicians (even if its heavily laden with soundbites and bullshit). A man is a human, as is a woman. Humans who can be born any sex or both sexes and it's not really anyone else's place to determine what they are or want to be, except theirs.

So shut up Rishi, et al.

Humans.

Ovaries before brovaries

I wish leslie knope
was my teacher in school
although I never much
paid attention to them
maybe just my fairy godmother
growing up in a world
where I was pitched
against my fellow girls
and they against me
that securing a boyfriend
was my ultimate purpose

girls are gossips
bitchy back stabbers
they will steal your beau
given half a chance
nothing about him
unable to keep it in his pants
poor men and their blameless testosterone

indoctrinated to believe
that other women
were our enemy
breaking free from this rhetoric
that was so intrinsically engrained

the women, wow
as I start to wake up
to this con I've been fed

through hardships through joy
big life decisions
in business and crises
through shared pain, health scares
partying, parenting, protesting our rights
messages on whatsapp late at night
brain dumps over hot mugs of tea
nods of understanding
acknowledged emotions
sighs of 'same, and me'
parcels in the post
filled with kindness and love
no occasion, a metaphorical hug

this millennial now gets it
why TV, teenage magazines at the time
drowned us with lies
to conquer first divide
oppress and control us
pinned us down with
all the emotional labour
but now we know together
we are a force of fucking nature

Week seven

current post hysterectomy recovery advice given to women (not strictly verbatim):

weeks one to two
basically you can't do fucking anything
just shuffle to the loo
no household chores
don't strain for a poo

weeks three to four
rest less, peel veg as you sit
light dusting each drawer
meander down the street
short walks but no more

weeks five to six
small pans to cook a little
maybe drive a bit
phased return to desk work
monotonous key clicks

weeks seven to eight
delicate gardening
aerobic exercise does await
fucking hoover and iron

unwanted domestic revival date

weeks nine to twelve
heavy loads of washing, sympathy shelved
supermarket shop guaranteed overwhelm
into your poor neglected vagina
lucky penis can now delve

if men had wombs and hysterectomies, their post operative care and healing guidelines would look like this:

weeks one to two
best you stay in hospital
we have a bed for your mum too
so she can look after
brave little soldier you

weeks three to four
full sick pay, bed rest and snore
beat the baloney pony
lest you have a backlog
of that virile sperm store

weeks five to six
new flat screen TV for his bedroom
stay active but go easy
nachos, dips and all the best biscuits

free sky sports thrown into the mix

weeks nine to fourteen
back to the gym for manly weights
just a nine hole golf tee
motorbike straddles, lawn mowing
into your wife man-seed sowing
extra fortnight, can't be too keen

so anyway the 1950s called and they asked for their recovery chart back because it reeks of misogyny and doesn't answer many of the questions I had in the weeks following my surgery. Now at seven weeks post op, I have put together my own updated version - because it's 2024 and I don't give a shit about dusting, peeling potatoes or aerobics:

weeks one to two
basically you can't do fucking anything
mainline laxatives, love heart sweets
endless mugs of peppermint brew
a lovely district nurse visits your house
to check on you*

weeks three to four
rest lots, recovery isn't linear
a few great days and you're active more

bad days are sneaky bitches therefore
delicious home made food
delivered daily to your door**
weeks five to six
more able now but be careful
hormones up to various tricks
disturbed sleep, eyes propped by matchsticks
masturbation externally is ok
and oxytocin is magic
no entry for fake or human dicks

weeks seven and beyond
(I don't know the actual answers to when these are ok, due to housework taking priority on the leaflets we are given, please don't take any of this as gospel truth)

hike a mountain, roller-skate, go on a zip wire
paint bedroom walls you had to stare at for weeks
lug logs for a fire, dumb-bells and deadlifts
carry a book-filled tote of feminist lit
dance hard in mosh pits
dildos or ding-a-lings (maybe start with just the tip)
stand up paddle boarding in the open sea
drag deckchairs into the sun
overthrow the mother fucking patriarchy

*this doesn't happen, but it should. It's so hard being sent home and not knowing what the hell is going on after major abdominal

surgery, infection risks, hormones in a blender
** likewise, because who wants to think about what to cook every damn day at the best of times

Boobs Glorious Boobs

When you have three older sisters that have grown their boobs, it sucks. Forever impatiently waiting for those first buds to appear, the holy grail of body lumps would soon be upon my chest. A chest that seemed to be the last of all my friends to still be doing its best impression of Wile E Coyote having met his fate, once again, beneath an Acme anvil intended for the demise of that bloody Roadrunner. My anvil flat, joke of chest. When would it be my turn.

Boobs are awesome, I loved looking at them before I was even blessed with my own. There's a distinct visual memory (imagine VHS tape quality) in the filing system of my brain, of when I first saw a topless model in a newspaper. It felt improper, if a little titillating. I knew at my age, I shouldn't be letting this overtly, semi-naked image of tatties burn into my retina, but burn it did. As would I burn... in hell, for my prepubescent, sinful, bi-curiosity.

It didn't stop there. Before long I was side-eyeing sunbathers on family holidays for another glimpse. Enraptured, enthralled and probably not very discreet either. In France, the non-British women always had their knockers out, all bronzed and glistening in the sun. Pancake Patty over here, still with my nothingness, started to muse. It must be so freeing to have as little clothes on as the men, boys, toddlers and the topless French women, in the sweltering summer heat. This stupid crop-top, bikini thing and for what? I didn't even have anything to cover and that boy over there, his nips were bigger than mine. All the unnecessary feigning distress, jumping and diving into the pool, just in case a swimsuit malfunction occurred and exposed me. Exposed what? A pair of pin pricks. The injustice of it all fired up my rebellion, powered by my impulsivity, a decision was made. I would free the nipple - decades before it was an actual campaign with it's own hashtag.

The wave machine cranked into action, rolls of piss infested, chlorinated water gradually ascending into fake waves. Adults, teenagers and children's heads were bobbing in and out of view as we jumped our mock, choppy seas. Mid undulation, just as the peak obscured me from all the human noggin buoys, I whipped off the top of my tweeny bikini. Water slapping at my chin and now bare, boobless torso. Hands to the sky, absolute joy and freedom plastered my face as I was being propelled higher before the next breaker descent. My lofty view now clear across the pool, nobody was batting an eyelid. They didn't give a shit.

Satisfied with the triumph of the mission, in came the return drop, my focus turned to the horizon, where

I unexpectedly lock eyes with someone poolside.
My dad.
Mere seconds passed but it felt never ending. That was undeniably a very mad dad face. There was only one thing left to do. Let the water swallow me up and scrabble back into my modesty. Submerged, holding my breath, both figuratively and literally. I panic-swam, mermaid style to emerge elsewhere. Clung to the side of the pool, shameful girly nips now out of sight - of course where they should be. Just hoping (begging) in that instant when the wave enveloped me, dad thought one of the following:

'I've had too many bacardis, I must be seeing things'
'Oh, that wasn't my daughter, that's mine over there, silly me'
'Oh no, the wave took her top, she must be so embarrassed'
Fuck my stupid joy on my betraying stupid face.

I genuinely can't remember the final outcome (thanks brain, forever my guardian) Neither of us have spoken of it since I got older either (and actually got boobs). That look on his face though, it still haunts me. A split second of disappointment and despair. I am fairly certain he knew was just the tip of the iceberg of what the future held for him; a good christian father, with me; his rebellious, rambunctious, fourth and final daughter.

Nope, I can't do this. There is no way I can end *boobs glorious boobs* talking about my dad.

Physically, I was a late developer, despite my brain and curiosity sitting a tad further up the development percentile. Who knows where the legend of stuffing tissues into bras originated. Probably Grange Hill or a show of similar ilk. I had been contemplating my life choices around this Kleenex dilemma, when as if by divine intervention, my mum and her friend levelled up from Tupperware selling (it could have been Avon or linens, I lost track). The newest evolution of the original housewives *Tupperware party* was now bras. Not your average C&A basics either. Flipping Gossards mate. No snot rags necessary, pure padded pretence.

I was giddy. Our dining table now lined with rows of moulded cups of varying sizes. Lace, smooth, black, white and nude. Not all were padded, mostly the early alphabet needed the extra help. The over-shoulder-boulder-holders, they had thick scaffold straps and I could fit both of my arse cheeks in one.

My sisters and I were allowed to pick one bra each before the women with actual hard cash arrived. Right at the foot of one of the meticulously organised lines (by size, colour and style) was the smallest black Gossard *padded* 28AA. Match made in heaven, it was meant to be and I didn't even care that my sisters were laughing at the label size. I was the winner here, this brassiere far exceeded any of their first ones. Mum couldn't even object to the *racy* black because it was the only one small enough. I bloody loved that bra and the insecurities it would now disguise. The first day I put that on under my white school shirt, was a day of pride. I finally had boobs (or at least appeared like I had). A hint of those dark straps through the cheap nylon, absolute goals.

Ironically, after all their piss-taking, yours truly ended up with the biggest boobs in the family. Size doesn't matter, I know, but let me have my moment.

Disco boobs

girls night out
on the town
skirt hems high
necklines down
pushed up tits
rest near face
bulging threats
of near escape

juicy jaffs
promise wonderbras
misty glittered
décolletage
tit-tape secured
spaniels ears
shaped in place
perfect spheres

arms dance high
to the air
jostling jugs
every pair
errant sweaty
chicken fillets
salty racks

pulsing mosh pits

chatter rings
through ladies loo
baps compared
with friends anew
girl-code nods
covert nip slips
banger doppelgänger
to kate winslets

in hooter hammock
phone resides
knocker pocket
cash safe inside
music stops
lights turned on
jubblies jiggle
shout one more song

tired tatties release
from brassiere
funbags swing free
without a care
smuggled raisins
in all their glory
bare-foot home… bounce norks-a-lordy

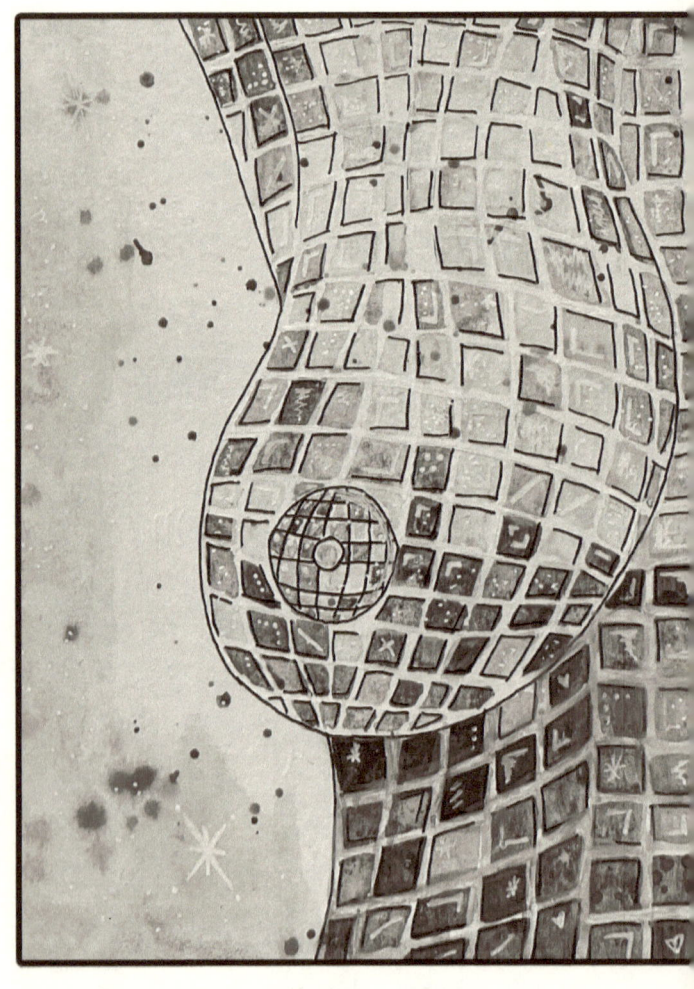

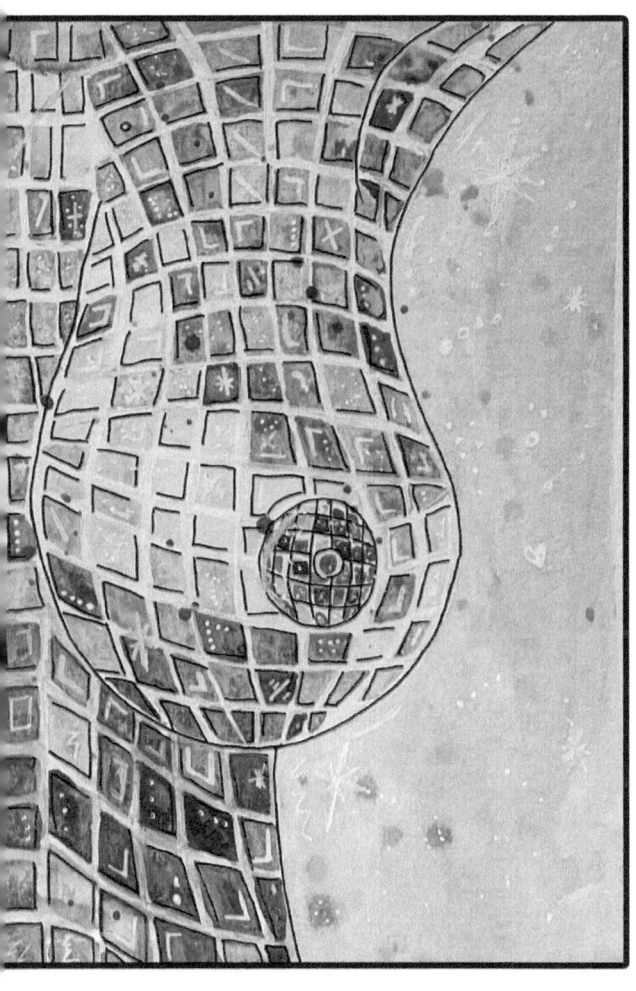

Magic mammaries

It would be remiss of me to write an entire section about boobs without mentioning how truly fucking magic they really are. Our bodies are incredible in so many ways but the fact we can nourish another living being inside and outside of us, well, it's worthy of an Olympic medal if you ask me. Modern society does not make it easy for women. My own breastfeeding chronicles consisted of three weeks for the first born, before shame halted it, just three days for my second (thanks trauma) and third time lucky, over two years of boob juice (thanks to six months of therapy).

I wish it was talked about more, not in the angry militant way it sometimes is. But openly, like it's the norm. I wish the community was there for all mothers, to enable them to hang about with a tit out - no drama. I wish there was support for the trauma endured by so many - trauma that can and does make breastfeeding a trigger. More importantly I wish the traumas weren't there in the first place.

The western world has right royally fucked post-natal times for us all. When we are brainwashed into 'capitalist individualism' over 'community' we lose the village to raise our young in. Our nipples have been sexualised and censored, full blown tyranny on the tits.

Sex creates babies, boobs feed babies - both are free and there in lays the systemic problem.

once inside cushioned core
through highway tether
her life and dinner laced

to baby bird like beak
lost latch off-course
clamps arm in hunger haste

bundled little cherub
nose to nipple guiding
eager pout now in place

small but mighty tongue
laps a let-down dance
upon elastic nip to taste

eyes roll as lids droop
lashes rest on apple cheeks
safe and calm embraced

tulip lips gentle snore
liquid gold dribble chin
sweet sleep a moments grace

thine magic mammaries
doth reign supreme
for she is absolutely tit-faced

Pillows

the perfect place
for little heads to rest
wrapped under your arm
cheek upon chest

four legged felines
scooch from your lap
buried head under chin
curled up boob nap

M&M nips

thousands of people
one milton keynes bowl
long summer solistice
knee length cargo shorts
paired with a bikini top
jumping and jostling
all day in the sun
waiting for the main act
who is really late actually

impatient drinks flying
where the fuck is slim shady
just as sun went to bed
sky began to weep
it poured and beat down
chill now bone deep
soaked to our cores
from the torrent above
out steps mr mathers

crowd elevates to roars
booming baselines
shivering in awe
damp chafing skin
rain soggy pockets

in each lemon triangle
harboured m&m nips

Polaroids

cookie cutter comparisons
to chests on screen
hours of music videos
gyrating cloned figures
living room dance routines
lubricating shots
lips loosened now free
warmed throats
by red and green

late night confessions
sisterhood shared woes
of low self esteem
because mine look lower
nips more biscuit than bean
self conscious when topless
are they *actually* saggy?
my body is broken
unmatched by the screen

refill glasses and bravado
lessons in gravity
of course bigger baps
sit different to ideals
in those magazines

whipping up her top
stood in solidarity
as we assess each other
atoning our hang ups
with laughter and clarity

a trio of bosom buddies
her, you and me
empowered in this moment
and it's dawning reality
each one of us varied
still valid human beings
all boobs are diverse
in your hype-girls, believe
every body is worthy
an assorted, eclectic,
intricate tableau scene

a feast of flavours
our unique set of genes
womankind a vision
a magnificent mix
a glorious, resplendent
tapestry of tits

These nights were the antidote to our self loathing, brought on from a barrage of 'perfection' in everything we consume. From such a young age we were led to believe that the female body had to look a certain way, with no consideration to the fact you have a genetic disposition to hips or tits, or even the lack there of. I'm so grateful to be surrounded by women who cheerlead each other. Navigating life in the noughties as a young woman was no mean feat!

The following instalment of this story, consisted of the three of us taking polaroids of each other. Through fits of giggles and spontaneous dances to, oh, I don't know, probably Shakira or Duffy as my sister and I rolled about the floor crying with laughter at Emma's very confident but very incorrect lyrics.

Then we sharpied messages on the photos to our significant others. Impulsively deciding what we really should do… is dig out envelopes and… there must be some stamps here somewhere. Fuelled with the confidence of mid-twenties women half a bottle of *Sours* shots deep and the affirmation of our kindred spirits. We each slipped our hot-off-the-press tit-pics into the now stamped and addressed, correctly correlating envelopes. A nice little Monday morning treat for our men from the postie. We were saucy little geniuses.

Bootylicious

'Does my bum look big in this?' the question I grew up hearing all the damn time. I didn't really get it. Bottoms are supposed to be round and comfy, surely? We have to sit on them. One of my sisters who was particularly slim, small framed and frankly very pretty, had a complex about her backside. I never understood it. To be fair, I was still sporting the physique of a pencil, given that I was a child.

There was a distinct lack in my child to young woman shape-shifting timeline. An entire chunk missing, due to the fact that I fell pregnant with my first baby at sixteen. No chance to see what insecurities puberty would bring me, because I was flung full throttle into pregnancy with no idea whether I had 'child-bearing hips' or not.

After I did bear child (growls in grizzly), I was able to finally discover my 'womanly' physique. I say womanly, I was so tiny and still just seventeen. With a teeny tiny waist sandwiched between my now curving hips and breasts straining under my juvenile skin. The midwife who told me 'being pregnant young has its advantages, your body will just spring back' was a fucking liar. The weight did *almost* immediately disappear. The body though, was forever changed and probably a little shell shocked. Despite my boobs look of 'just been titted-up by Edward Scissorhands' fresh red stretch-marks a-go-go, I was a big fan of the new silhouette my frame was now casting. Baby got back. No matter the fluctuations over the years on the scales, my waist to arse ratio has remained that way. Curves at last.

The whistle-stop tour of said transition was fresh out of any stops and more like a white knuckle death-drop ride at full pelt. Leaving me zero time or space to be prepared for what owning 'an arse you'd like to smack' would mean attention wise. There has been unsolicited smacks a plenty too. Possibly the most memorable (if somewhat *WTF*) was when I started a new job at twenty one. Innocently stood at a high workbench having IT training on the internal working components of a computer. My head down, listening intently as, let's call him 'Steve' imparted his geekdom upon me (I was expected to sell graphics cards, processors, memory and the like, to actual companies who wanted to build computers). We were in the zone and my brain was loving the information upload hyper-focus. When my new boss, a stranger, in my new job, walked past me and apparently could not control the impulse of slapping my derrière. Computer Steve and I rendered speechless for a moment, in utter disbelief, just looked at each other mouths open like guppies.

Boss man stuttered a bit as he sheepishly and very quickly left the workshop.

In an era of 'heroin chic' being the coveted body type, my bootie bucked the trend. It had never particularly bothered me per se. However, the bombardment of images thrown at me from celebrities, did start to wear a little. Especially when it came to getting a pair of jeans that fit my peachy cheeks in. They always gaped wider than the Dartford tunnel at my lower back, a void between waistband and flesh. Still to this day, I struggle to get trousers or jeans to simultaneously fit my waist and bum properly, although it is a little better. I'm embracing the elasticated waist and thank fuck low-rise is no longer the norm.

The concept of body shape being a fashion trend is mind boggling to me. Imagine my delight though when I travelled to Uganda in 2012, for volunteer work with my mum. All I had to do was traverse continents to be in fashion. Mum and I stayed with an incredible power-house of a woman. But even power-houses have their hang ups and she packed her clothes with patootie padding, for fear of being taunted for her flat *Mzungu* bottom. Then, there was me, an actual Mzungu - the name for white foreigners - being stopped and admired for my arse by Ugandan women. They literally couldn't believe this fair faced, English woman, had the apparently, very sought-after, protruding round rump of their nation.

Arse logic

pain in the arse
someone or something
is very much trying one's patience

arsehole
self explanatory,
synonym of obnoxious twatfuck
BMW driver, middle-lane hogger
not to be mistaken with…

arseholed
really, very drunk, should not have started on shots
impulse control is in the bin
there may be vomit or a kebab, or both
the room will spin

arse about
the act of doing something and nothing.
'just going to arse about in town for a bit'

kick up the arse
in the virtual sense rather than literal
a motivation of sorts

kick-arse/kickass
double hard bastard like karate kid

cool as fuck, spectacular and most impressive

got your arse kicked
you were dealt a whooping either by actual combat
or the recipient of a severe telling off

arse about face
there's been a mix-up, you've got your jumper on
backwards, you're not *kris kross*

arse over tit
silly goose fell over

hanging out your arse
a monumental hangover from too much booze
the regrettable upshot of being absolutely *arseholed*
the night before

face like a cat's arse/smacked arse
pouty lipped sulk, grumpy little twat

rat's arse (couldn't give one)
don't care, no fucks left

rat arsed
see also arseholed
swaying pisshead

kiss my arse
piss off, you mean nothing to me

arse kisser/licker
teacher's pet, fawning for scraps of attention or appreciation from an apparent hierarchal person brown nose

half arsed
they are not satisfied with your minimal effort
'half arsed attempt'

can't be arsed
cba - underwhelming lack of motivation
probably needs a *kick up the arse*
teenager

tight arse
cheapskate, doesn't share or spend
probably northern

smart arse
not necessarily intelligent, just a back-chatty little shit

shove it up your arse
the bullshit your peddling isn't being bought
off you fuck and take it with you

Patriarchal Pants

tell your daughters
tell them not to listen
to what the magazines
or the shop fronts say
the catwalks and media
for the ones that are pushed
are designed by or for men
what else could explain
the Topshop thongs circa 2002
tiny triangles of polyester mesh
splitting your arse in two
threats of thrush
disguised in neon pinks
see-through bonnet
must display minimal pubes
cheese wire chafed ring piece
VPL shamed celebs
god forbid visible pants
pointless little bows
cheap itchy lace
seams separating flaps
synthetic materials
rub at delicate skin
hearts and flowers
promises laid beneath

ignore it all
vaginas are magic
they even self clean
a finely tuned ecosystem
should be adorned
in a soft vulva cradle
peach cheeks free
protest against spandex
embrace butt dimples
let the pussy breathe

Under-bum

Laughter for me is like a skeleton key to my body that can crack through the awkwardness. Unlock each doorway to bypass my hang ups with some joshing, well timed one liners or a cheeky tickle of under-bum. It makes my brain fizzle with delight. There are enough things in life to be serious about, so for me, intimacy should not be one of them. I mean, I *seriously* want orgasms, but to get there I need to be charged by chortles to fire up the dopamine, serotonin and endorphins. A person that can have me uninhibited, in absolute stitches, is a very sexy human indeed.

The first time I woke up in my now-husband's bed could have been a morning of cringe, shame or regret. We were colleagues, a line very much crossed. He made me laugh at work a lot. That morning as the alcohol had been slept off, he dissolved my hangxiety with a generous dose of wit, charm and tickles. There was no longer a sense of being an embarrassed naked mistake in a colleagues bed. He'd made me feel sexy and content, like that was exactly where I should be. Safe. That shit really gets me going.

I *accidentally* went home in his boxers, of which, once washed and dried, I surreptitiously returned via the second drawer of his desk at work accompanied with a teasing post-it note. I knew full well, when he discovered it (in our very open plan office), he would panic at being caught, hopefully laugh a little and be reminded of that first night we had.

trace my lines
warm hugs with laughter
flesh caress
brush my shoulder

quick-witted words
bookend nibbled lobes
giggling ribs vibrate
played by lips and nose

sturdy hands grasp
impatient jerky hips
heart linked humour
skin by fingertips

curved grade-a-rump
sweet delicious peach
booty under-bum
where borders meet

inside jokes
joy sealed beam with kiss
beneath derriere cheeks
secret tickly bottom bits

Who Is She

When you have three sisters, a mum and are also a female yourself, you'd think growing up, we would be pretty sorted on the anatomy between our legs, right? Wrong!

For years in our house it was called a *neath-there*. A what now? My eldest sister, adorably called her vulva and general vaginal area, a toddler rendition of 'underneath there'. Which transpired when being taught personal hygiene skills and important body parts to wash. This stuck and was passed on to the rest of us because I guess it was easier than calling a sin-purse by it's real name. When I was pregnant with my first daughter, I tried to wrack my brain on what my parents actually called our vulvas when we were little. Or even, when we were too old and no longer able to innocently whisper *neath-there* without it being very weird. But nope, I don't think they ever did provide an alternative.

Therefore my vagina education came from the school playground. Headfirst into fanny, muff and minge. Not literally, calm down. Learning what I could from whatever teenagers were gossiping about wasn't a fast-track pass to genital wisdom, just in case you were wondering. But boy did I hear some shit. Shit, I might add, I knew nothing about. Beside the knowledge that I definitely could not, would not, ask my mum or dad what a *blow job* or *wank* were. Didn't have the internet to ask either, not even Jeeves. It was simply a case of smiling and nodding along, hoping to outwardly channel 'sex-literate, whisker-biscuit aficionado'. My internal filing system was hungry for data, inhaling post-it-note nuggets of information at any and all opportunities, so as not to appear like a Mormon.

On the subject of wanking. I had garnered from my aforementioned research, that boys had wet-dreams and no that did not mean they pissed the bed whilst dreaming about having a wee (yes I did that once or twice). Also that boys apparently can't leave their little prawns alone. It's a sin to purposefully play with it but everyone knows they do - because they're boys.

Girls however, no mention of them and their wandering hands to explore the mysterious *she who shall not be named*. In fact, at one point in my early teens my sister and I had been ill-advised (source unknown) that if a girl did partake in self-play, it meant they loved fanny and ergo were a lesbian. Which by the way, we knew by now, was also a sin.

My Vagina is...

adventurous
beautiful
cosy and cute

delicious
excellent
friendly and fun

she glows
hot and horny
irresistibly juicy

keen as a kitten
lick-able lips
magically majestic

a naughty
outstanding
perfect pussy

she is quality
radiant, robust
soft, serene

terrifically tasty

underestimated
victorious vagine

she's wonderful and warm
sometimes X-rated
yes yes yes orgasmic and zen

Crikey that was a mission. I don't think we've ever managed to get to the tail end of the alphabet when playing this game before. If you've never played it, I'll summarise. Usually reserved for long car journeys or camp fires with innocent themes such as animals or countries. However this one, yes, you've guessed it, the theme is words to describe your vagina. I believe this version is a firm favourite for hen nights or Ann Summers parties. Absolute cringe central. However a few years back my sisters and I started a semi-tradition of getting together with our mum for mother's day, without the kids and to generally kick back, massages, nibbles, hot tubs and wine.

This was in the days before I had an 'off switch' with alcohol and frankly a spot of child-free, day-time drinking meant we quickly sunk several bottles between us. Mum is not a drinker. She loves a couple of glasses but we set a precedent that she would never keep up with. Needless to say, the days of not having a proper word for our vulva and vagina growing up was paid back in full as we underwent much hilarity in the form of the alphabet game.

Front-bum fire

peer pressure is a mother fucker
women waxing lyrical
about smooth bonnets
chanting razor free sonnets

here is my lady, she's incredible
gets right in there
til front and back
soft, shiny and bare

dutifully arrange a session
of lunch-break torture
flaming fandango pain
and back to work again

Read my lips

bow down
chow down
savour the flavour
each semiquaver
expertly riff and repeat
make me sing to the beat

take your time
enjoy the ride
take a break
peel paper back
tease away foil
part at the crease
nibble at edges
don't rush this treat

rub my lamp
for magic
is hidden inside
lap my dish
elixir of honey
full to the brim
a goddess within

dine in my gorge

tour my ravines
bathe in my springs
perch on the brink
here wash your face
in my little pink love sink

worship the fruit
juicy and ripe
suck the sugar
each little bite
be gracious
and patient
an honour you'll see
to the deity
one bends the knee

pressure and pleasure
considered rotation
will reward your endeavours
a standing ovation
a delicacy ready
for you to explore
rich and delicious
wanting for more

throbbing and yearning
coursing with heat
sit at my table

indulge in my feast
marvel the creature
tongue will unleash...

...the secrets she would whisper
if these clam lips could speak

Trusty Ticker

The heart. Why do we associate this organ with love? A bloody mass of chambers, muscle and tissue that thumpity thumps blood and oxygen from your head to your toes. Why not our brains? home of the pituitary gland, the actual secreter of oxytocin, the *love hormone*. Which I have just discovered, sits at the base of the brain just behind the bridge of our noses. Valentine's cards with 'I *NOSE* YOU' are giving cute pun vibes that I am totally here for. Although I'm a little less confident with the nose equivalent to the classic heart shape that has been depicted as the icon of love (the internet tells me it was a French dude that started it in the 1250s). Please also note, that until the fourteenth century it was originally upside down. Little ball-bag of love.

The truth is, the heart manifests physical reactions to our emotions. To our big emotions. From racing beats of giddy excitement around the person that makes your fandango flutter. To visceral aches of grief and pain, ergo, heart break.

Heart idioms have long perplexed my autistic brain, phrases like 'she has such a big heart' or 'he wears his heart on his sleeve' when describing someone's character. Surely personality is built in the brain. An overly large heart would be cause of serious medical concern. Also having an organ on the outside of one's body, pinned to a garment, is just idiotic at best. That thing literally keeps you alive, best to leave it in it's pericardium pocket and locked safely behind your ribcage. Does that make a heart-sleever an ignoramus? I thought it was supposed to be a compliment.

Which segues me into my next notion on the onus we grant upon this important cardiovascular organ. Bear with me on this one. If the brain is truly where our personality and character forms, with it's glands and hormones, it's critical thinking and so forth. Then why is it that our hearts carry the weight of life or death, of love, hate or heartbreak? If our heart stops, we die. None of our other limbs or parts can work without it. Our brains cannot function without the oxygen from the heart. Yet we can be brain-dead and our futile heart continues it's job. No judgement or perception, no purpose, no soul. Just a living organism. A house plant. Our hearts keep us alive but it is our brains that give us the ability to love and care. It is our brains that make us human.

Literal thinking aside, I am dedicating the start of this chapter to the people I love.

Long before I had the hair-brained idea of collating my

poetry into a book and now a second book, penning poetry was not just a way for me to process the gazillion open tabs in my brain but also my love language. Platonic love, family love and of course to my other half too.

You will have to excuse the slap-dashery of the following poems because they haven't been through the fine-tune-it-for-publishing-o'meter and I don't want to change them. Although, I do confess, to using poetic license (ha!) on the titles, due to these personal verses originally being (mostly) un-labelled. Some are poems for big life moments, anniversaries or birthdays, others are just because.

This is me, my heart, loving my people.

My first friend

my first friend
my best friend
my run around the room
and shout crazy words friend
you cut my hair off
I mated your hamster with another
roller skating and bike rides
pretending to be dogs
singing alanis loudly together
on long dark walks home
puking up spaghetti
out the window on holiday
please don't leave me Gemma
a solid rendition of
Irish dancing to bewitched
the best laughs
the best dancing
the up all night talking
raising our boys together
how has it been twenty years
the giggles and all the tears
you are my best friend
you were my first friend
I love you even when you're a knob
I love you without end

You made a grug

you have your ticket now to the club
it's pretty cool in here, we stay up all night
talk jibberish because our brains are mush
love and oxytocin wave after wave
rush after rush

no silly, not that kind of club
it's one you join when you first do that test
nausea and excitement overwhelm you
your heart beating into your chest

you've done it!!
you've successfully gotten impregnated
top job to you both, good S.E.X skills
you've reproduced and procreated

you're making a little human all of your own
it's cells split rapidly time after time
going from weird little alien head
to a little tiny baby, using your belly as a home

you sit and imagine what little grug will look like
first you choose all your best features
from him and from you

then roll around the floor laughing as you imagine
your long neck, his chest hole and bandy legs too

none of it matters as you grow that child
tucked up and safe in your womb
a body inside your body almost ready to meet
as it grows bigger and bigger
with not much more room

a message for your miniature being;
we cannot wait to meet you for the very first time
a piece of your mum and some of your dad
not long little one, until we can see your round face
I've no doubt you'll not just be brilliant
you'll be all kinds of ace

Dick tracey

climbing a tree as high as we can
knowing you will get us down when we
realise we don't have the correct descent plan

winding us up before bed and buckeroo
you going AWOL and after a search
finding you hiding in the study or in the loo

late nights pretending to be asleep
as you play cards with friends
a total sore lose and an exceptionally
ungracious winner, a comical cheat
the fun and laughter never ends

swimming trunks worthy of a museum
lilo competitions, teaching us how to *dunk*
me accidentally dunking the wrong dad once

that time we swapped the broken dining chairs
for yours, you really did not find it funny
not one little bit
all of us thinking it was the best prank
we ever did commit

taking us into work with you and letting us play

us using the internal phone lines
making important calls
mega giant colouring book photocopies
made our day

endless patience watching our
'performances' at home that we put together
as sisters to impress you
terrible singing, awful acting
not just us but you too!

you are a massive geek
and over the years you've coded us
times table programmes on the amstrad
and been an overall nerd dad

you didn't know it but thanks
for the secret stairs code
we could quickly dash and turn off the TV
our post bedtime crime
once we heard that throat clearance
and creek of the steps, two at a time

being atop your shoulders was
the best place in the world to be
you would shout 'DUCK'
because of low hanging branches

I always looked but never found those ducks
I took it quite literally

small and awkward, I was not a confident
swimmer by any means
I really wanted to try and swim
underneath the catamaran boat
we swam together
I did it because you were encouraging
and helped me believe

you are never too far away
from the next project or mini grand design
whether that's at your own house
or one of your daughter's houses
just be careful of those ladders
you might not bounce next time

we converse respectfully
from religion to politics
even if we don't alway agree
I enjoy those summer evenings
in the garden with wine
listening to you debate so passionately

when your two youngest daughters
became mothers so young
you helped us raise our boys to actual men

it's no coincidence were in Jake's first phone
as 'grandad awesome'

it warms my soul when you
take the time to call James
after interviews or to play golf
when his own dad was taken from us too soon
you check in, step up
in your heart there is plenty of room

if I were to sum you up into one sentence
it would simply be
you're the kindest man I've ever known
I strive to be as good
and I hope that this attribute is reflected
in my own children and also in me

Every day I'm jostling

it's not often you meet a person
you know you will be connected to forever
and when you do you keep them close
a wonderful specimen a precious treasure

through the twists and turns
of this life an adult rollercoaster
we stay in touch no matter how long
the laughter and love for one another

games nights, spa trips, London lunches
the riches of our time spent a total pleasure
career changes, big moves
fond memories of all our time together

no matter how far away we are
life with you in is infinitely better
one day we will be face to face again
jocelyn my most amazing hugger

Matriarch

hair plaiter, sandwich maker
organiser of picnics in the park
the sun to our solar system
our small but mighty matriarch

you nursed us when sick
with cuddles and lucozade
'just a sip'
grazed knees and plasters,
pink stinky germolene
you worked like a maid
but to us you were queen

popcorn in silver dishes
dripping in syrup, angel delight,
france with hot chocolate in bowls
chinese on games night

we could make you crumple
with a tickle of your knees
through the tears and the laughter
you would cry 'no, stop, please'

you always put our needs
ahead of your own

you ate the burnt toast
so that none went to waste
you, cooked, cleaned and baked
until we were all fully grown

dressing us all up together
our outfits the same
even though you weren't the
best at getting the right name

holding hands trying to keep up with you
as your heels tapped a clip clip
the blow away lilo on holiday
and your hilarious cockney accent slip

a style icon through the years
the biggest glasses I've seen
poodle perm curls
mascara combed in your fringe
blue and green

if you were a barbie doll
your accessories would be
an impeccable outfit with
matching shoes, bag and jewellery
some crochet and chocolate
and of course a bottle of Bacardi

unwavering support when
we had our own children too
babysitting, moving back home
solid as a rock, nothing phased you

limitless love and charity
that knows no bounds
kosovo, uganda, opening your home
blankets and clothes,
smartie tubes full of pounds

you raised us and taught us
gifts of motherhood you did impart
we are the suns of our own solar systems now
but you will forever be
our magnificent matriarch

Day one

my rock,
my ride or die,
thank you
for being my unwavering support
and a life line
despite the miles of roads between us

I feel very lucky
to have been born
with a ready made best friend
to play, learn and grow with
you are my
day one best friend
my person

I love you

The big ten

you proposed to me on a winter's day
with Erin in my big round belly
what else was I going to say?!
as Ed was asking my dad for Nicola's hand
he'd planned his surprise for Christmas day
you jumped the line the week before
without 'permission' which made me love you more
a rebel feminist, living in sin
on my finger you popped a beautiful ring

we had what was considered
a long engagement to allow for the birth
of Jake's much wanted 'older brother'
a birth so profound and loving with you there
a second time round of me becoming a mother
on all fours as you fed me lucozade
like a baby goat

I'm not sure how, but we really did
raise not one but two amazing kids
she was not quite what Jake had in mind
ok a sister and much younger
but she loved Spiderman was funny
sweet and kind

we raised them both in our very first house
and when we weren't being 'mum and dad'
we threw the best parties we'd ever had
my relentless need for fancy dress
you jumped in with both feet
and without protest
superheroes, punk party, black and white
burlesque, london underground,
zombie apocalypse
with amazing friends,
we partied hard through the night

not ones to shy away from adventure
with the help of wedding gifts
we bough that loveable rust bucket Lola
driving around on a constant high
that crappy old VW made us nothing but smile

losing your dad was such a tough time
but he taught us that time was so precious
and we could live better lives
renovating then living in his old home
enabling us both to retrain
for the greater things to come
we both jumped shop from the monotonous rat race
without a glance back and a super smug face

if he could tell you now, I know what he'd say
in his thick Yorkshire accent,
bushy moustache and out of his mouth
he'd tell you he's proud
even if you 'sold out' public education
and moved too far south

moving house once more
new village, school and people
my photography business taking off
your teaching going from strength to strength
planning more new adventures
another and another
road trips across Europe
memories to last a lifetime
our beautiful vow renewal
feet in the sand reaffirming to each other

and when we were least expecting it
and incredible surprise
you were sleeping and I said
'babe I'm pregnant'
you soon opened your eyes

little miss Mila moo, our magic number
you stole our hearts and our slumber
not one, nor two but three pretty cool humans

we've nurtured and watched
each one blooming

lets not beat around the bush
some days are real hard
we wish the years would rush
we wonder what it would be like
for a little more freedom
they then say 'I love you'
'mum you're right'
or simply hug us tight
we embrace the time
years please don't rush
we can watch you grow
so utterly proud and turn to mush

the latest instalment of adventure
for us walkeroos
upping sticks, moving south
to be able to hot-foot it to the beach
whenever we choose
paddle boarding, camping,
lazy days in the sun in our garden
old friends coming to stay, new friends made
doing it all together

I love you even when
you are looking at another bike online

I love you even when
you try to be quiet (which is impossible)
I love you even when you are annoying
I love you even when you
are a jabby-damp-towel, swamp-donkey, cup-of-tea

I love you because
you love me even when I'm annoying
I love you because
you love me even when sometimes I don't love myself
I love you because we fit, we work
we are a continuous tag team
of needing a rock and being the rock
of pulling each other up from below
and then pushing each other up higher

I love you because we are the adventure

Tit club

friendship is…
dropping donuts at the door
floor picnics and inappropriate movies
waiting for babies to be born

memes exchanged in late night chats
cups of tea propping sleepless heads
space to share when kids are twats

comfort plain for all to see
over shares and laughter lunches
boobing bebes, nipples free

photos, frolics, toes in lakes
dinner movies, fire pits
books shared, ample Jaffa cakes

bell tents camping, minor peril
face gems, hair flowers, hippy days
grubby children wild and feral

spends enabled, impulsive crafts
fossil finds, sea dips, ice creams
poems recited and autographs

feminist rants, parenting and politics
no holds barred, no judgement
verbal dumps when men are dicks

reels back and forth, tiktoks too
each app a different tangent
homework catch-ups scrolling through

Emily
my mate
has all the things
a joyful, chaotic
loyal human being

Care and Action

The three words that rom-coms would lead you to believe are the most important thing to hear, are not, in my opinion the magical elixir of words that many hold them to be. They are too easy for (most) people to utter. Don't get me wrong, when truly meant, they should be said and said often. Above all they only ever hold any gravitas when accompanied by supporting actions of care. *Newsflash*, if they are held back from you as a weapon to make you feel worthless, to watch you crumble and left wanting, needing validation, this isn't love either. A favoured tactic of one of my psychotic ex-boyfriends, who didn't want me but didn't want anyone else to have me either.

My first 'love' was the tiny blonde boy, who joined our junior school mid-year. We became a solid double act with our mutual love of nature and spending hours on end scaling fields and trees. Bike rides, fishing for newts and watching hedgehogs at dusk. Me, the weird feral girl, with muddy bruised knees and a naive, uneducated understanding of the world around me. Especially when it came to friendship etiquette and romance. And him, the confident, small but cute, curiously intoxicating newbie. Evidently, unrequited love treacherously oozed out of my every pour, because he 'friend-zoned' me early on, but I didn't care. I just wanted to be near him. To be dazzled by his enigmatic presence for as long as I could, even as his oddball, tomboy, bestie.

The day I discovered his family were moving away and he would subsequently no longer be at the same school as me, was one of my earliest memories of heartbreak. More accurately described as the total devastation of my soul.

Cue the following tableau of angst. Rolling around on the floor of my bedroom in a pool of my own snot and tears, whilst wailing out Whitney between wracking sobs of grief and cradling my light-grey soft toy kitten. Frantically pushing at the clunky buttons on my tape deck as the track finished. An awkward and agitated pause in my otherwise very raw display of emotions. I had to rewind this absolute banger, the only suitable song to portray my turmoil.

Click. Play. Cry.

'I have nothing'. Sniff.

Wail and repeat.

My ten year old, tender heart, understood why the heart is the official mascot of love. Laying there on the scratchy god-awful dusky-rose carpet. Tears dribbling into my earholes from my face, over and over. An immeasurable agony of pain in my chest as if it had been punched through, ripped out and squeezed by

Satan himself. His bloody fist clenching my broken heart aloft, in front of my eyes.

The connection of love is not exclusively for romantic adorations. Nor, dare I say, humans.

My non-human love and heartbreak goes back to even earlier than hedgehog boy. My heart was bestowed to a toy. A doll. Not just any doll, but a 1980s Rainbow Brite doll. She had a soft body and plastic head. Honey golden locks in the form of woollen strands, tied up on her head with a ribbon bow. The coolest knee-high rainbow boots to match her puffy rainbow sleeves. The sleeves were topped, of course, with very ostentatious eighties shoulders. Iridescent, probably highly flammable, futuristic (for back then) pointed shoulder pads, to twin with her cool shiny skirt that finished into an arrow shaped hem. Oh and her face was joy personified. Cute cartoon eyes set far too wide apart and a button nose between her round cheeks. If you're a millennial too, you'll remember when dolls weren't painted with slutty faces. None of those exaggerated cat-eyes with winged eye-liner, brash eyeshadow and massive lips emblazoned in a bold cherry reds. No, Rainbow Brite had a modest mouth in a muted pink and the most adorable smile. One lone, subtle, lilac star printed on her cheek for a little extra magic.

Hours were spent setting her up on the Colour Cottage. This too was soft and padded. Like a suitcase in a way. The flap folded down from the arched rainbow to create the garden, where I arranged dinner parties with Twink on the plastic furniture. Admittedly, the cottage was reminiscent of a baby's play mat. Imagine an infant's jungle gym with sensory toys dangling from the arch as they lay there batting them, the odd dribble and gurgle, kicking their legs out and having no control of their jerky movements. Yeah, kind of like one of those.

So I *half* understood why mum did it. It's a bit of a blur now, given my age and also the trauma of realising my mum had given away my beloved doll to the school jumble sale. Why not just give the cottage and leave me her. Why? And why not talk to me first? I'd have said, take the cottage, take any of this fisher price crap, but pleeeeeeease, leave me her.

'But she's a soft doll, you're too old for soft dolls now'. Five year old me had a total breakdown.

We marched back up to school to be first in line for the sale. With a fist full of meagre coins, I was frantic, searching the table tops to buy her back. Where is she? Lashes threatening with shiny blobs of tears, ready to roll. I spoke to some of the adults behind the tables and no-one had seen her. Which means whoever sifted through the bin-liners donated by parents, must have kept my precious doll for themselves. Inconsolable. And never, ever forgotten.

My sister bought me a Rainbow Brite t-shirt one birthday in my twenties. Years and a couple of children later, I bought another t-shirt in a bigger size. Wistfully, I would sporadically scroll eBay for a replacement doll but they were always so overpriced and I just couldn't justify spending that on a toy as a thirty-something.

All now in our forties, a few weeks ago, my sisters sent me a link to a newly released version for sale in the shops. A monstrosity! What had they done to her. So with a rage induced vigour, I started trawling Vinted and picked up an original 1983 Rainbow Brite for an absolute bargain. She hath arrived and exactly the same but twice the size of my original one. Her once honey golden hair, no longer tied in a bow, just limp and hanging matted around her face. Remnants of leaves and twigs à la Mr Twit, lodged in her barnet, hands and legs. She was grubby, had the distinguishable whiff of 'dusty attic' but she was salvageable and still had her original dress.

Both my husband and kids, bore witness to my face lighting up as I retrieved her from the battered cardboard box. My inner child's cup of joy runneth over and shone in my eyes. Taking my precious cargo upstairs for some quiet time, I sat and lovingly restored her for over six hours. That neurodivergent hyperfocus bringing all the goods to enable me to utilise whatever I had to hand for the job. Gentle cleansing water (usually for my make up removal) and soft cotton pads as a starting point. Meticulously and carefully cleaning away decades of grime. I picked out detritus, undressed her, wiped down her clothes. Smashing my way through half a pack of cotton pads and forgetting to eat or drink for several hours, I looked up some videos online to tackle the hair. Bored and impatient with those videos, I decided to opt for a careful sink shampoo without submerging the soft body. Once washed and dried, I sat for a few more hours and painstakingly separated every single strand of hair, rolling them between my fingers, to twist the wool back to its original state and delicately snipped the end of each, wisp by wisp. My youngest daughter popped in occasionally to check on my progress or to watch for a while in awe. I tasked her with sourcing a ribbon from the craft stash and now was the final moment. Dress back on, hair returned to her iconic high ponytail and a shiny new ribbon in place.

I can't stop looking at her, she's perfect. Am I weird? An adult woman cooing over a doll like this? Well, apparently not, according to the ninety-eight-thousand TikTok views and a comment section filled with similar childhood traumas of lost or given away beloved toys. Yes I did record the process and post it for others to share in my joy, and I'm not alone.

This is your sign. You can buy a child's toy as an adult with your own money if you want to.

Back to those words. I love you. I was musing over them and the subtle signalling of aforementioned care and affection. Those little things that mean so much, without the need to sing at me like Buddy the elf to his biological Dad.

When James and I were a fledgling couple, I suffered pretty terribly with nightmares (thanks trauma) and no, not fitful flashbacks of me reaching out for a 10" soft-bodied child's doll that was ripped away from me at such and young and regrettable age. We're talking, scary back-alley running from narcissistic exes. My subconscious had cultivated them into irrational fear monsters that sent my heart galloping at lightening speed. Except my legs or hands wouldn't work properly. During this particular nocturnal episode of internal torture at the hands of my own bastard brain, I made it to a phone box. In theory this was a win. Usually I'd be flailing in slow motion as impending doom enveloped and aggressively pressed down on me, before waking up screaming. I digress. Back to the phone box. It's dark and desolate, mist hanging as low as the kerbs. I've managed to momentarily shake my assailant from my heels and reach the box. I'm stabbing at the numbers with my fingers, my parents house phone, no answer. Then I lift the receiver again and go to call James before realising, I have no idea what his number is *off by heart* (another senseless idiom about hearts). In the real world, I'm clearly thrashing about and groaning in my sleep. James comforts me. As I wake and through the sounds of my heart pounding like a freight train, I tell him that evening's account of horror from the shit show of my mind. Holding me close, he gradually calms me back to a regular rhythm and begins to recite his phone number. Repeating back and forth between us until I remember it. It has been permanently lodged in my brain thereafter. Twenty years on, my heart makes its presence known every time I have to scratch those digits onto a form with a biro. Just casually detailing my next of kin or emergency contact for the kids and my chest pulsates. A quickening and little dance from my heart in recognition of when those numbers were gifted to me in a pure, unadulterated, act of love.

Instagram may have you fooled into thinking grand displays of aesthetic balloon arches, matching pyjamas, massive bunches of florals and birthday gifts spanning thirty days, are the gold standard of heart felt actions and expressions of endearment. Yes, I enjoy receiving gifts. Do you know what else makes me feel loved, appreciated and valued? Being accompanied up the M6 motorway to visit my best friend at university because he understands the love between her and I, is no less important than the love between him and I. Random union bar dance-offs and conversations with people he barely knows because he knows they are my people.

Him laying my phone on the side of my face, balanced precariously on my ear because I'm too hungover to move but I need my weekend thirty minute chat with her. Then popping to the shop to get me fruit pastel ice lollies because my mouth feels like I dined on camel arse in my sleep. Hand written notes telling me how proud he is that I'm flying off to Uganda for charity volunteering and all the fundraising and passion I put into it. Words of support in a card with a *100* pin badge for my first centenary of book sales. Happily supporting me in my endeavours which sometimes can be a bit inconvenient when we have a family. Willingly climbing out of our bed and sleeping on the sofa, so that I can hold and comfort my sister through something as she sobs herself to sleep. Suggesting a fancy dress outfit swap, curtailing my total meltdown. Because my carefully curated Amy Winehouse outfit was 'ruined' due to me misplacing the temporary tattoos I found on eBay and hated myself for being useless (undiagnosed ADHD). I was now bedecked as pretty naff Freddie Mercury at the 'Hair' themed celebration, but the joy I got transforming James into a spectacular Amy, over-rode everything else. Being a constant, a hype-man, growing with me. Following me with a tape-measure when I've started another impulsive interior re-vamp. Sending me articles on my special interests. Playing me Warren G 'Regulate' from YouTube on his phone because he knows, I'm dysregulated and that laughter soothes me. Texts from work just to say hello, because he's thinking of me when we aren't together. Listening to me when I have something to say, really listening, digesting and processing.

Again, I won't turn down a new house plant or well considered and thoughtful pair of earrings. However, without all the nuanced, understated gestures, consumer gifts are as fulfilling as a Big Mac is to your body when what it really needs is an array of nutrients to flourish. You don't need a million-lumens-powered projector, to shine your love virtue like the bat signal over Gotham, for all to see. Just do good, be good. Care and action.

Platonic supersonic

tell your friends
tell them that you love them
tell them their worth

let them know
let them know your life is better
with them in it

soul mates
are not limited
solely for romance

so tell them
let them know

Not transactional

When I delved deep into my soul, to decipher the connection between those I hold absolute dearest to my heart, it was evident. Almost stupidly obvious why. It doesn't matter how long since I last saw them - at my age my closest are often geographically the furthest away. But it's irrelevant. It could be six days or six months since we've breathed the same air and every single time feels the same. An ease, a peace, that envelopes me when I'm around them. The human I married, my sister that is a part of me, not just through blood. The allied friendships that know me and I them, to our cores. Absolute fucking treasures.

friendships, lovers
connections to be true
not born of convenience
simply you

effortless company
clouds depart
shoulders loosen
mutual therapy sipped tea

heirs and graces
left at the door

masks redundant on hooks
authenticity

a glimpse of your face
pops of joy
crackle in my heart
a radiant little glow stick

gravity keeps us
in each other's orbit
our momentum balanced
just so

souls tethered
through time and space
illuminated worth and wonder
jewel pocked clear night sky

a want to be near you
not for what you can give
but for who you are
we are not transactional

thou shalt not
collect points, redeem vouchers
cash in your chips
no club-card swipes

you exist
and I love you

the golden hour sunshine
on a crisp autumn day
the fresh line-dried sheets
and newly shaved legs
the art and laughter
indulged through splendid cities
the song in the car
that I know every word

you are contentment
you are brilliance
and you are home

Cranial Chronicles

Have you ever given your brain much thought beyond whether or not you could achieve the grades you wanted? Whether you have a natural aptitude for math or more of a tendency to doodle in the margins? What about your brain health?

The discovery and chronicles throughout my first book, were all about my autistic and ADHD brain post-diagnosis. It was a wild time. It was intense and confusing. There was a catatonic un-packing of a lot of shit.

There's an unfathomable rhetoric about 'labels' when people seek assessments and diagnoses. As if they will hinder or tarnish. Yet, understanding how my brain works, why it functions differently to the general population, has without doubt, saved my life. The torment I have endured throughout my years, even of my own doing, has been because I didn't know my brain. I spent so much time inside my mind, fighting against and not working *with* it. Perpetually setting myself up to fail and then hating on myself for being a failure.

Worst still, I self-medicated to try and feel normal or to drown out the little gremlin in my skull. Do you know what deteriorates your precious brain health? Deprecating self-talk and alcohol. After a solid eighteen months of exploring the inner workings of my grey matter and forgiving it's little nuances, in place of chastising them. Slowly but surely, I began to let go. Brain and I were no longer enemies but were tentatively becoming actual friends. Like a neglected puppy I was rescuing. I had to gain her trust. Feed her, take care and love her so that she would flourish and overcome her previous traumas. Therapy, appropriate medication for the ADHD and finally breaking up with my toxic partner - alcohol.

It's funny, I don't ever remember being taught how to look after my brain. I do remember every single time I was told I should be thin and pretty. Quiet and compliant. How to work as hard as I possibly could and always strive to work harder and earn more, spend more… be more. There's a fuck-tonne of *unlearning* taking place. The little inner-skull-gremlin is still there sometimes, but brain and I are holding hands now. Embracing the good and facing the shitty bits stronger together. I heard on a podcast recently: 'should is just could with shame attached' - it hit deep and I urge you to also work on eliminating *should* from your self-sabotage arsenal. So what, I am chronically disorganised at domesticity, who cares, not me. Do you know what my mind is capable of though? Turns out, more than I ever thought, ever believed possible.

Hello brain

for forty years
my brain was hidden
in a shadowed recess
tucked
in the airing-cupboard of my body
somewhere under the spare towels
and long forgotten linens
each word I had written
every page began a beautiful unravelling
I wasn't expecting

I'd emptied out the cupboard
and inside found a gift
a present that was meant for me
so many years ago
stashed and lost accidentally

hello brain

no longer in the confines
of that musty corner
silenced
by the tick and hum of the boiler
cradling my prize
I brought her out into the light

and what a sight…

my magnificent mind

What's on your mind?

what's on your mind?
everything and anything all of the time

a wife and a parent forever laden with guilt
planning adventures for this life that we lovingly built

not least is the worry, the ambition, and the 'should's
walk in my thoughts, chase squirrels, lost in the woods

there's the good and the bad and ugly too
the cacophony torrential all the world through

from one to the other a flick of a switch
and days when this brain is a bit of a bitch

pride can be buried by each slur ever said
expectations and pressures they weigh down this head

but I love this impassioned, complicated me
though sometimes my thoughts are a wild place to be

Mindful Misophonia

a clock with no tick
is it even a clock
its face presented
for all to see

in this home
we're divergent
to fit in our world
each stroke
must be silent

poor clock
true self hidden
alone on the wall
hands moving
mute and compliant
acceptable

I pause and observe
each second passing
rotating time
frustrated that yet again
clock has slowed

dragging its feet

falling behind
pondering its place
true nature held back
this voiceless face

has its battery
run down quicker
through resisting its norm
stifled timekeeper
unable to communicate
energy drained to conform

now I'm sat
contemplating
the double empathy theory
an analogy appearing
with this analogue piece

would allistics
burnout in a world
made for autistics
or is the silenced dial
sluggish from masking
is it one of us

disguising its stims
echolalia suppressed
clock's spoons depleted

authenticity feared
here I am penning poetry
condolences to cogs
aware my affinity…

                                        is all a bit weird

Wonder

if my brain were a photo
the image developing
full, bold and shining
beautiful wonder by five
light and joy in details
no matter how small
there is so much to see
colours and character
unadulterated glee

passing through the years
wonder loses it's way
an ink-jet printer copy
to thin plain paper
left in a frame by the window
where the outside world
begins to bleach and fade
impression starts to wane

pressures to grow up
misplaced priorities
this humble life is finite
discarded scrap of wonder
we simply don't have time

awe now lay beside the bins
rain beaten with responsibility

neglected wonder overlooked
a lost and lonely toy
packed up in the attic
left behind at the curb
dirtied by the bustling highway
the boxes in the garage
damp and battered across the years
demands and disappointment
war, hate and grief

a secret you should know
wonder is not obsolete
for brain still has the negative
please just take a moment
you're still allowed to play
value isn't in the hours worked
curiosity and daydreams
enrich in every way

stand still

   breathe deep

watch the sky with delight
read books

dance in the sea
brush paint onto canvas
sing and touch the trees
life may well be brief
but my love
no matter how old
you grow to be

that magic
    there's so much more

set your wonder free

Profit and Loss

I need to tell you something. Yes you. I'm talking to you. How do you feel now, about your body? Have you reflected at all about the trap that we have been lead to? They want us to hate our bodies. Who else are they going to sell to if we just accept them?

From the land of our ancestors before us, carved up and profited. The water to quench and sustain us. The stunning views gated by carparks with charges galore. Stripping earth's rainforests for profit and greed. Even faith has a price, from tithes and unquestioning belief. Industrialised food, sold back to us, processed and shit. It costs us our earnings and also our health. Wrapped in plastic they then tax us to recycle or trash. Homes built each smaller with nowhere to grow, so allotments to rent for somewhere to sew. Children packed off to schools not fit for purpose. So they can make us all work, to make them all richer. Our brains pumped with ideals from every direction. Brainwashed to believe in this manmade competition. Too busy to stop and just enjoy life. You must earn more and buy more so that your face, your clothes, your house and your body look *their* kind of right. Fast fashion, fad diets, snake oil by the gallon. Chastised for your fat yet peddled consumption. Spinning a culture of that well deserved drink. When connection is craved but the weight of the labour, the crushing state of the world, bills and beauty regimes, weary bodies from the drudgery, all leave us unable to think. But you must squeeze in a brow tint and a buff body wax. Subscriptions and memberships, credit cards to the max. Glue on eyelashes, cut at your skin. Fill up your lips, buy that product and this, contour your nose and your chin. Guasha your jawline, red-light mask your whole face. You must look effortless and natural, you disheveled disgrace. No hip dips or muffin tops, wrinkles or marks. Buy Spanx, fuck it buy software to clone out your pores, force your tits into bras. They package kudos and fame in a box tied with lies and deceit, songs for stadiums, art for investment. All the while we are here, just chasing our tails, lemmings following the crowd. Your body is just fine, what you need is more time. Time to spend with your family and friends. Time to laugh and sing. To feel the sun warm your skin. To watch spring flowers uncurl as they decorate the world. Tell stories and use your body to nourish your soul. It is all there if you stop, take a break and resist their distractions. Hating and admonishing your body at what cost? Someone else's profit and your loss. Wear whatever the fuck you want, sing out of tune just for fun. Be a mess, make mistakes, ask for what you want during sex. Stop performing and conforming, be more free. Your body is your vessel and life is the journey. You're allowed to enjoy it, because you are so fucking worthy.

Acknowledgments

This isn't my first rodeo but it feels so weird writing a gratitude speech, like an imposter on stage accepting an award.

I began writing *Belly Button Champagne Pools* very swiftly after I finished writing *Mess is Progress*. What I hadn't banked on was it taking so long to finish. My life took several swerves not listed on my bingo card. Starting with home educating our youngest daughter and the disappearance of any and pretty much all time to myself. On top of that, major abdominal surgery, of which I was very naive about recovery and a year later, I'm still left with chronic fatigue. You might notice the influence of such time in the *Sabotaged By My Baby Box* chapter. I will say, the post anaesthesia induced insomnia did bring out some great two am writing sessions. Swings and roundabouts and all that!

My first thanks goes out to the friends who rallied around me in those recovery days. New friends from the home ed community, old friends who sat on the edge of my bed with cake on my birthday. Even once the worst was over, it was pretty hard to face writing what was supposed to be my 'fun book about the body and life', when my body was currently not my friend and my life was effectively on pause. But I kept going, piece by piece.

Thank you to the lovely ladies in my local library who encouraged me to speak with the county head office about my first book. That resulted in me being invited to do an author talk and Q&A session to launch the Somerset Libraries brand new Neurodiversity Collection. Poetry was always something I had in the quiet of my notepads and mind. Standing in front of an audience and sharing my poems spurred me on to have more belief in myself. I treasure the wonderful feedback notes I received from the attendees.

Thank you to the glorious Angie who runs *She Speaks*. I was so nervous attending this women's poetry group in a bookshop after hours. Listening intently as each person shared their crafted words before plucking up the courage to stand there and share my own. It felt bloody incredible. Next stop - an open mic poetry night (shits pants).

My hype team, who have endured my monologues and recitals as this book grew. From reading aloud to them, voice notes and random screen shots of poems. Emily, (also top marks for crying when you read one at your birthday dinner!). Gemma, Pickle and Justine who feature heavily in the antics that built the foundations for many of the stories, of which are featured herein.

Sara and Jamie who I first read *Not Transactional* to in a Taxi to the airport at the end of our trip in Barcelona. An attempt to soothe our panic in traffic and the possibility of missing our flight. The best trip ever and of course it inspired a new line for the poem.

My kids, two of you aren't really kids anymore. Jake I'm so proud of you and love our little messenger chats and yes one day I will be reading a poem at your wedding. Erin, you could be placed in many of the thank you paragraphs. Your unwavering support during my surgery recovery, my hype girl and here in my pride. Mila, in home educating you I have learned so much myself and about who I am, what I really like. Thank you for opening my eyes and my world to so much more. You are awesome.

James my steadfast rock, cheerleader and number one partner in crime. Every time I evolve or switch direction you go with me. Forever the stabilisers to my inner child's bicycle.

www.ingramcontent.com/pod-product-compliance
Lightning Source LLC
Chambersburg PA
CBHW020523080526
44583CB00013B/708